Walid Siti

Exhibition view *Re-Construction*. Solo exhibition at Edge of Arabia, London, 2014.
Courtesy of Edge of Arabia. Photo credit: Alex Maguire.

Exhibition view *The Black Tower*. Solo exhibition at Zilberman Gallery, Berlin, 2017.
Courtesy of Zilberman Gallery. Photo credit: A.R.Laub.

Installation view *Phantom Land*, 2017. Hard board, foam board, plaster of Paris, grout and acrylic paint.
5 × 700 × 900 cm. 13th Sharjah Biennale *Tamawuj*, Sharjah, 2017. Courtesy of the Sharjah Art Foundation.

Nat Muller (ed.)

Walid Siti

KEHRER

Table of Contents

Walid Siti:
An Art of Lived Experience, Forms and Fabulation
Nat Muller
14

War +
Conflict

Dohuk to London:
A Tumultuous Journey
Venetia Porter
20

Landscape +
Architecture

Walid Siti:
Landscape, History and War
Zainab Bahrani
74

Belonging +
Exile

Tracing Constellations:
Belonging and Exile in the Practice of Walid Siti
Sarah Johnson
144

Artist Biography
190

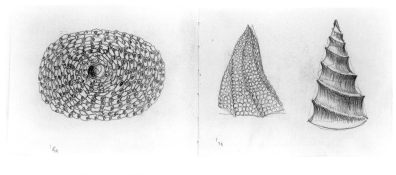

↗ Study from sketchbook, 1999. Pencil on paper. 14 × 38 cm.
↗ Study for *Tower* series, 1997. Pen on paper. 18 × 40 cm.
↑ Artist installing his work *Anatomy of Climbing* at Edge of Arabia, London, 2014.

Walid Siti:
An Art of Lived Experience, Forms and Fabulation

Nat Muller

Nat Muller is an independent
curator specialised in contempo-
rary art from the Middle East.
Recent exhibitions include
Spectral Imprints for the Abraaj
Group Art Prize in Dubai (2012);
Adel Abidin's solo exhibition *I
love to love … * at Forum Box in
Helsinki (2013); *Customs Made:
Quotidian Practices & Everyday
Rituals* at Maraya Art Centre in
Sharjah (2014); *This is the Time.
This is the Record of the Time*
at Stedelijk Museum / American
University of Beirut Gallery
(2014/15); the A.M. Qattan 2016
Young Artist of the Year Award
at Qalandiya International in
Ramallah and The Mosaic Rooms in
London; Walid Siti's solo exhibi-
tion *The Black Tower* at Zilberman
Gallery Berlin (2017); Hera
Büyüktaşcıyan's solo exhibition
*Neither on the Ground nor in the
Sky* at ifa Gallery Berlin (2019).
She was Associate Curator for the
Delfina Foundation's Politics of
Food Program in London in 2015.
She has curated film programs for
Rotterdam's International Film
Festival, Norwegian Short Film
Festival, International Short
Film Festival Oberhausen and
Video D.U.M.B.O New York. Her
writing on contemporary art from
the Middle East has been widely
published and she edited Sadik
Kwaish Alfraji's first monograph
(Schilt Publishing, 2015) and
Nancy Atakan's *Passing On* (Kehrer
Verlag, 2016). Her AHRC-funded
PhD project at Birmingham City
University researches science
fiction in contemporary visual
practices from the Middle East.
In 2019 she curated the Danish
Pavilion with Palestinian artist
Larissa Sansour for the 58th
Venice Biennale.

Walid Siti has had his studio in the London borough of Hackney for close to thirty years. Sketches and drawings are affixed to the walls and lay piled up on tables along-side tubes of glue and paint, brushes soak in cut plastic bottles, boxes are filled with twig, string, cardboard and other materials. There are prototypes and models, bubble wrap, works ready to be shipped across the world, exhibition catalogues and numerous unfinished cups of tea. A closer look reveals that certain images fill, even haunt, this place of work: the mountains and rugged landscape of the artist's native Iraqi Kurdistan,[1] the characteristic Mesopotamian architecture with its ziggurats, and the violence of war and conflict that has tormented Iraq for so many decades. The sorrow and pain that exile has brought Siti, since he left Iraq in 1976, is never far away. And yet, this studio is a place of magic where every single sheet of paper, careful brushstroke and meticulously put-together object means more than the sum of its parts. Siti's art is as much one of lived experience and form, as it is one of fabulation.

There is so much more to Siti's forty-year career than can be summarised in one publication. Yet, this book is an attempt to showcase his oeuvre by focusing on what I would like to call his grammar of forms, meaning the visual tropes and conceptual lexicon that have accompanied him over the years and continue to shape his practice to this day. Rather than considering the book's thematic sections, respectively on war and conflict, landscape and architecture, and belonging and exile, as entities separate from each other, they are an invitation to view how entangled these concepts are in Siti's work. This is wonderfully exemplified in Siti's sketchbooks in which he has repeatedly captured and permutated the spiralling ninth-century minaret – the Malwiya – of the Great Mosque of Samarra, north of Baghdad. The iconic tower is a recurring motif in Siti's work; it speaks to architectural ingenuity, craftmanship, divinity, but at the same time it is reminiscent of human hubris, the Tower of Babel, and leaving one's mark on a landscape. In these sketchbooks we also find mountains morphing into ladders, and conversely ziggurats into mountains. These structures are anything but monoliths; Siti has rendered them porous. In his sketches on brown packing paper he has deconstructed them to their units of form (squares, cones, triangles, rectangles); they bend and sway and have acquired movement. In paintings such as his Mountain series (2010) and Dialogue of Towers (2013), sturdy towers and mountains seem propped up by a fine mesh or scaffolding of paint. The monumentality of their presence has become pixelated and ephemeral. In sculptural works like Ceremonies (2016), Imprints (2016) and The Black Tower (2016) the Malwiya is coated in thick black paint, as if tarred. It is overrun by an army of tiny plastic soldiers and lies on its side, collapsed and broken. Siti salutes the magnificent architectural heritage and natural landscape of Iraq while at the same time pointing out the dangers of bowing to any form of ideology and taking iconography at face value. His mountains and towers are in essence wounded images and their capacity to represent a singular idea of power is shattered. As such, Siti's projects take on a quality that is both commemorative and foreshadowing.

Politics and poetics mix seamlessly in Siti's practice. He has a penchant for working with cheap, mass-produced and throwaway materials such as cardboard, used newspapers, and other discarded bits and bobs. This was first borne out of thrift when he settled in London as a young political refugee in 1984, but he is also fascinated by the possibilities these materials afford him to fabricate something meaningful out of nothing. The Poundshop, not far from his London home, remains one of his favourite art supply haunts.[2] Take the wall piece Stone Tales (2018) that was first shown in Yerevan. Here Siti has crafted over 800 card-folded squares, lined with Kurdish, Arabic and Armenian newspapers. Together they represent a mountain. As he writes in his artist statement 'each crevice holds a history.' It is also an example how these different stories can link and translate across geographies. For Siti this carries echoes of Mount Zawa, Shada, and Faroun, the majestic mountains overlooking his hometown of Dohuk in Iraqi Kurdistan. In Armenia and its diasporas one of the most potent symbols of belonging is Mount Ararat, just across the Turkish border. Narratives of exile, dispossession and political histories come together here, and the humbleness of the material induces empathy, rather than awe. Another example demonstrating the use of materials is the installation The Silver Lining (2013) in which strands of barbed wire are pulled across a mirror. Here one of the most deterring and violent materials, used in war and at borders and other crossings becomes something multi-layered. The mirror reflects a distorted and incomplete image of the viewer. It is brutal but also fragile. We are drawn to our own reflections but confronted with the barbed wire's dividing lines and how it functions as a separator between inside and outside, inclusion and exclusion. As viewers we become implicated in this dynamic of boundary-setting. Of note is that this work was first shown in an exhibition in Diyarbakir, the unofficial capital of Turkish Kurdistan. Coming of age as a Kurd in Ba'thist Iraq, Siti understands first-hand what exclusion means.[3] In her contribution Venetia Porter traces

how Siti's journeys through art and life are marked by the turbulence of Iraqi politics, from growing up in Dohuk, his student days at the renowned Institute of Fine Arts in Baghdad in the early 1970s, continuing his studies in the former Yugoslavia, to his exile in London. Siti's oeuvre has always been propelled by the politics of place, whether he has found himself back in Dohuk on family visits or as he engaged with Iraq and the region from afar.

Writing on what it means to produce art from the diaspora, Iraqi artist Rashad Selim observes that '[a]rt in this state of disjunction treads an uninsured path through the grim landscape of loss and exile. And yet [in this art] can be found a will to express an essential humanity and love that counters reactionary pessimism; a creativity opening on to a vision of transformation at best and the preservation of significance at least.'[4] This sentiment is articulated throughout Siti's practice but most palpably in his site-specific works. Depending on where and in what context he creates these projects, they take on different meanings. Monument to the Unsung (2018), on the fringes of Amsterdam's city centre, takes on a memorial function that insists on the oft-marginalised presence and subjectivities of women. Another example works with the more controlled exhibition space of the gallery: a small sketch of a ladder is flipped horizontally and transformed into a wall-sized mural, turning the ladder into a fence. Or an intervention in Dohuk's public space takes the form of a public condemnation as in the recent project Cut and Paste (2019), in which the artist decries the relentless neoliberal real estate development in Dohuk. And sometimes, like in an iteration of The Tower (2015), a seven-metre high installation of twisted lattice overlooking Istanbul's waterfront stands defiantly in all its vulnerability. In her contribution Sarah Johnson describes how in Siti's work a dynamic of presence and disappearance is always at play and that his contorted ladder installations and towering structures often preclude climbing. It is indeed this tension between the aspirational and the futile; between ruination and hope that makes Siti's work so very much of our time and that resonates with the humanity Rashad Selim refers to.

Over the years Siti has included an array of mediums and techniques in his practice. From drawing, painting and mixed media installations, to most recently video. The thicker and heavier brushstrokes of the 1980s and 1990s such as seen in the War series (1986–90) and Tormented Landscape (1990–96) express the carnage of the Iran-Iraq War, the massacre of Kurdish civilians, and the atrocities of the reign of Saddam Hussein; they show the work of an artist in mourning. Later works retain the sense of loss but translate the essence of violence in a more abstracted manner. Longing and belonging gradually find a place. The love Selim refers to is manifest in every single piece, but perhaps best seen in series such as Precious Stones (2004), Family Ties (2004–10) and A Perfect Formation (2012–14) in which family and the relationship of the individual to the collective take pride of place. Here a delicate spiritual energy unfolds from the centre to the periphery of the composition and in some of the works the shape of a mountainous landscape shimmers through. In her essay for this book Zainab Bahrani shows how deeply Siti's art is rooted in his connection to a place 'that is there and not there.' A place that he maps with love and trepidation. This book is an invitation to enter that fraught world.

1
Iraqi Kurdistan and Turkish Kurdistan are also known as Southern Kurdistan and Northern Kurdistan.

2
See for Siti's use of material Nat Muller, "A Certain Aesthetic: Walid Siti in Conversation with Nat Muller," in: *Ibraaz*, 20 March 2017, https://www.ibraaz.org/ interviews/215 [last accessed 23 February 2020].

3
The Ba'ath (Resurrection) Party gained a growing influence in Iraq after the 1958 revolution, which overthrew the Iraqi monarchy and resulted in the Republic of Iraq. In 1968 the nationalist Ba'ath Party secured power in Iraq with Saddam Hussein as its strongman; he would become president in 1979 till the US-led invasion in 2003. The Kurds of northeast Iraq had long been neglected socially and economically by the central government in Baghdad. Like other minorities Kurds were forcibly displaced and culturally Arabised by the Ba'ath regime. Anti-Kurdish policies and reprisals against the civilian population combined with severe repression and economic blockades were particularly egregious during the Iran-Iraq War (1980–88), including chemical attacks and the genocidal Anfal campaign in 1988. See for historical context Albert Hourani, *A History of the Arab Peoples* (London: Faber and Faber, 1991), 404-17, 434. Also see Martin van Bruinessen, "The Kurds Between Iraq and Iran," in: *MERIP Middle East Report*, No.141, Hidden Wars, Jul-Aug (1986): 14-27. For the Anfal campaign see "Genocide in Iraq," in: *Human Rights Watch*, 1993, https://www.hrw.org/ reports/1993/iraqanfal/. [last accessed 25 February 2020].

4
Rashad Selim, "Diaspora, Departure and Remains," in: Maysaloun Faraj, ed., *Strokes of Genius: Contemporary Iraqi Art* (London: Saqi Books, 2001), 47.

War
+
Conflict

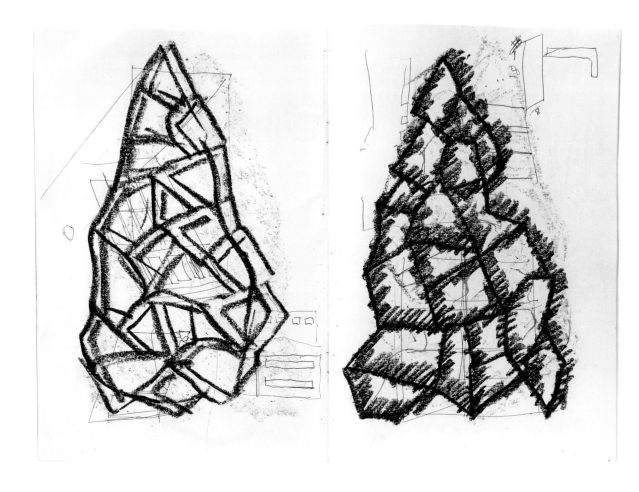

↑ The artist in his first year of art study, Baghdad, 1971.
↗ Artist, middle bottom row, with group of students
  at the Institute of Fine Arts, Baghdad, 1972.
→ Study for *Mountain series*, 2013. Pastel on paper. 29 × 41 cm.

20

Dohuk to London:
A Tumultuous Journey

Venetia Porter

Venetia Porter is a senior
curator at the British Museum
for the collections of Islamic
and Contemporary Middle East
art. She studied Arabic and
Persian and Islamic Art at the
University of Oxford, and her PhD
from the University of Durham is
on the history and architecture of Medieval Yemen. She has
curated two major exhibitions at
the British Museum, *Word into
Art* (2006) and *Hajj: Journey to
the Heart of Islam* (2012) and
was the lead curator for the
Albukhary Foundation Gallery of
the Islamic World (2018). Her
research and publications range
from Yemeni history through
Arabic inscriptions and amulets
to contemporary art. Her publications include *Arabic and Persian
Seals and Amulets in the British
Museum* (2011) and contributions
to *The Islamic World: A History
in Objects* (2018). A book on
the British Museum's collection
of the contemporary art of the
Middle East will be published in
autumn 2020.

Walid Siti's story reads like a political history of Iraq in microcosm.[1] It is an uncompromising story of determi-nation, rebellion and hope, of family and strong friend-ships; a story in which the making of art has acted as the continuum along a journey that has taken him from Dohuk, which in the early 1950s was 'a small city on the edge of confrontation' to London, where he now works and lives. From a Kurdish family with a strong sense of social justice, Siti's father, Mohammed, had established a trade union in Dohuk. With communist leanings, though not directly affiliated to the communist party, he was fre-quently detained during the 1960s in prisons across Iraq.

Siti recalls the six-hour train journey with his remarkable feisty grandmother, 'a social figure in the community,' to visit him in jail in Baghdad. This was a moment within a period of revolt and then outright war between the Kurds, who were fighting for regional autonomy, and the govern-ment in Baghdad, which lasted between about 1961–70.[2] 'Three of my father's friends were hanged in the town square' Siti recalls. 'A terrific dancer but useless at busi-ness,' during much of Siti's young life his father was hiding from the authorities in a village in the Kurdish mountains with the National movement in Iraqi Kurdistan – until 1970 when a truce was declared. During his father's absence, Siti and his four siblings were looked after by their mother, Amina, and an uncle. 'My mum was everything for us.' His empathy for women comes from his admiration for her: 'women are the unknown soldier.' This led him recently to make Monument to the Unsung (2018), an installation in which are placed dozens of names of Kurdish women – who are named after flowers, mountains, rocks or the sun.

At school in Dohuk, his affinity for art was quickly rec-ognised, and he recalls two art teachers Nasir al-Din and Anwar who encouraged him, even letting him off sports to work on art projects. By the time he was sixteen, the decision had been made to study art and after a rigorous exam, he successfully enrolled in the Institute of Fine Arts in Baghdad. The next five years between 1971 and 1976 were a glorious period for Siti personally although the politics of Iraq would grow increasingly bleak. The Ba'th party (the name means Renaissance) came to power in 1968 with Saddam Hussein elected vice-chairman of the Revolutionary Command Council in 1969. As described by Charles Tripp: 'The emergence of Saddam Husain and his construction of a dictatorship demanding obedience and using violence on a scale unmatched in Iraq's history were the dominant themes of this period.'[3] Siti's years in Baghdad coincided precisely with that increasingly re-pressive hold on the population and, as Siti recalls, as

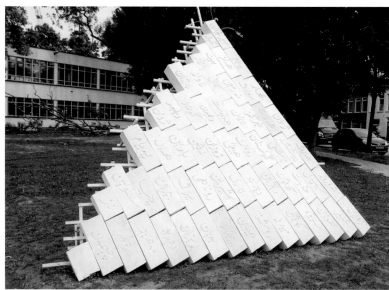

↑ The artist at his studio in London, 2008.
↗ Artist at work. London, 2014.
→ *Monument to the Unsung*, 2018. Site-specific installation.
Aerated cement block and pine wood. 300 × 400 × 300 cm.
Pay Attention Please! at Public Art Amsterdam, 2018.

time went on, it became necessary to demonstrate loyalty to the party. The Institute of Fine Arts at Baghdad University, formerly the Music Institute established in 1936, which had expanded to include art with Faiq Hassan (1914–1992) heading the Painting Department in 1939, was where the major figures in Iraqi art were affiliated, from Hafidh al-Drouby (1914–1991), to Jewad Selim (1919–1961) and others of his generation who studied and taught there, and later, artists such as Hanaa Malallah.[4] Highlighting his 'leftish background,' but coming from 'a very conventional setup' as Siti recalls: 'The atmosphere was really wonderful, people coming from all over Iraq … many of them were not Ba'this, they came to do art.' Outside of class, the students had a real sense of social engagement and they would go to cafés, to the <u>suqs</u> (markets) and draw. As supporters of national liberation causes all over the world the students were heady with socialist ideas; fervent supporters of the Palestinians, against the Vietnam war, anti-Imperialist: 'We were young and hot-blooded.' They made posters, and Siti's block-printed images that have much in common with German Expressionism, convey that raw energy that he expresses verbally when he speaks of that time.

The course at the Institute took five years. The first three consisted of general art, sculpture painting and ceramics. The last two years were the moment for specialisation and Siti chose graphic art and printmaking in particular. The teachers he remembers with the most fondness and respect were Shakir Hassan Al Said (1925–2004) and Rafa Nasiri (1940–2013), both towering figures in the Iraqi art scene: Shakir Hassan Al Said (along with Jewad Selim the creator of the Baghdad Modern Art group in 195) and later the practitioner of the theory of the 'One Dimension' from 1973, and Rafa Nasiri, one of the major printmakers of the Arab World.[5] Another teacher Siti knew as 'Mr. Haqi' who had studied in East Germany was also extremely influential, and in the class which consisted of about fifteen to twenty students, they learnt all the printmaking skills from etching to block printing.

In response to a question on the impact Shakir Hassan Al Said had on him, Siti describes how Al Said's work, characterised by abstraction, the use of the letter, the influence of mysticism, was not for him and his fellow artists who were more interested in politically engaged art. Despite not following the same artistic path, however, Siti and his friends respected Al Said enormously and in his classes they learnt about art history, and specially about the importance of <u>turath</u> (heritage). Interestingly, unlike the previous generation of artists – that of Dia al-Azzawi

(b.1939) for example – his group did not spend time in the museum, studying and drawing Sumerian sculpture and other objects pertaining to the ancient civilisation of Iraq; something he now regrets.

The end of the course in 1976, where he received second prize for his work, presented Siti with a crucial moment of decision and his choices were: to go to the Academy of Fine Arts 'but I was not a Ba'thi' (and nor did he intend becoming one), to join the army, a definite no, or to go and study abroad. The fact that he would not join the party was increasingly becoming a problem: members of the party were everywhere and he recalls being physically threatened in his hall of residence, when he supported a friend who had put an image of Lenin in the background of a block-printed poster.

The most appealing option was to leave Iraq, although not being a Ba'thi meant that he was not able to obtain a grant to study abroad. He had to find his own means to do this and he managed to muster $600. A group – Hamid Tahir, Azad Karim (also Kurdish), Ghaleb Ba'ei and Siti – headed for Yugoslavia; the closeness of the two countries meant that they did not need to obtain a visa. They ended up in Ljubljana and the story that now emerges is complex: it involves questionable extensions of visas, personal stories of friends who could not cope with separation from the homeland, the pervading and unsettling reach of the Ba'th party, involvement in student politics and a first marriage, the kindness of strangers and an extraordinary network of support provided by what was a great revelation to Siti – the numbers of like-minded Iraqis living outside Iraq. Accepted for free by the Ljubljana Academy of Fine Arts, the four Iraqis spent the first year studying Slovenian before furthering their studies in art, supporting themselves with all manner of jobs. He briefly returned to Iraq to see his family in the summer of 1977 – he had always intended that he would obtain the degree and return to help his family who needed his support. He was not to return, however, for another sixteen years.

The Academy of Fine Arts in Ljubljana was known for printmaking and two mentors now emerge: Bogdan Borčić (1926–2014) and Zvest Appolonio (1935–2009). Siti was content in Ljubljana and began exhibiting his work. However, the reach of the Iraqi government was long, he was under scrutiny both by Ba'thi informants and the local police. 'London was not in my plans, but it happened that I had a Kurdish friend there.' Arriving in London in 1984 armed with a return ticket to Belgrade, it was only through the intervention of Jeremy Corbyn, Labour MP for Islington North, (leader of the opposition 2015–2019) that he was allowed into the UK and, after two years, was finally granted asylum. In London, he worked for his friend Simon Cham'oun who had an interior design business, he studied English, took courses in printmaking and quickly found his feet through the Iraqi network. He cites in particular, artist Dia al-Azzawi and the moral support he gave him at this time. Also, key was artist Mahmoud Sabri (1927–2012) who lived in Prague but would frequently visit his daughter in London and see Siti: 'we corresponded and he was a great support for my early shaky days in London.' The breakthrough in London occurred in 1987 when he met curator Rose Issa who was then organising exhibitions at the Kufa Gallery owned by the Iraqi architect Mohammed Makiya (1914–2015).[6] The exhibition included Siti and his two friends Hamid Tahir and Azad Karim from the Baghdad–Ljubljana days who had remained in Slovenia.

The 'shaky days' that Siti refers to above was a period of massive sustained turbulence for Iraq; the Iran-Iraq War 1980-88, the campaigns by Saddam Hussein against the Kurdistan Democratic Party (KDP) and Patriotic Union of Kurdistan (PUK) in Kurdistan in 1987, the beginning of the Anfal in Kurdistan (literally meaning 'spoils of war', this was the violent campaign to reassert government control led by Ali Hassan al-Majid), and the chemical attack on Halabja in 1988; the annexation of Kuwait by Iraq in 1990, the beginning of Desert Storm and the bombardment of Iraq in 1991, the imposition of sanctions on Iraq, and finally the US led invasion of Iraq in 2003. The War series of the late 1980s and the series Tormented Landscapes (1991) reflect this period.

Siti, in the early part of this chronology of conflict, was living with his close friend the poet Raad Mushatat: 'he took me in into his family.'[7] Mushatat, a Shi'i from Baghdad, was part of a group of anti-Saddam activists. They would watch on television, angry and helpless, the tragic effects of the latter days of the Iran–Iraq War and later the Anfal. But Siti's sense of guilt was profound, watching the events unfold from a safe distance: 'most Iraqis even now have this element within their psychology, the feeling of guilt at not having been with those people who have suffered in this way.'

These relentless images were the genesis of Dark Interludes (2001). From the War series made in the late 1980s, at the encouragement of scholar Kanan Makiya,[8] thirteen prints were selected to be made into a portfolio.

It is in these works that Siti's 'vocabulary' can be seen to have coalesced: the 'symbols' as he describes them of ancient Mesopotamia, of the Islamic era and that of Saddam: ziggurats, the Abbasid era Malwiya, the evocations of power in the palaces, and threatening creatures stripped down to essentials without sentimentality. Contrasting the works with Goya's Disasters of War, in his moving preface to the work, Makiya comments: 'this is a world darker than Goya's, in a little studio in London … he [Siti] worked alone and unknown consumed by the need to come to terms with the darkness that was closing in on the land of his birth.'[9]

As the darkness over Iraq continued to unfold Siti grew more reclusive, his reading confined to existentialist literature – reading and re-reading the writings of Friedrich Nietzsche (1844–1900). In 1992, he returned to Iraq after sixteen years. It was following this visit that he changed his name from Walid Mustafa (which appears on the leaflet of the 1987 exhibition) to Walid Siti to honour the family memory. Siti was the name of the formidable grandmother, mentioned above, and his father although named Mohammed Mustafa was always known as Mohammed Siti because of her. She had died in the Kurdish mountains in 1991 while fleeing Saddam Hussein's army in its attack against the Kurds after the uprisings following the Iraqi forces' expulsion from Kuwait in 1991.

These last years have seen Siti return regularly to Iraq. He has made public art and given lectures in Dohuk; he has participated in projects in Erbil and Sulaymaniyah, he has climbed the Malwiya of Samarra for the first time. He wants to re-connect and he is optimistic about the future: 'there are talented people, there is hope … for me this is a dimension that I have been longing for.'

5

The theory of 'One Dimension' evolved out of Shakir Hassan Al Said's move from representation to abstraction in which he drew on Sufism and existential philosophical ideas. This was combined with his belief in *istilham al-turath* – 'seeking inspiration from heritage.' The goal was to arrive at a 'truth,' and, from 1958 onwards his inspiration was the Arabic letter and the line which he incorporated into abstract compositions. *Al-Bu'd al-Wahid*, the One Dimension Group, gathered artists including Jamil Hamoudi and Madiha Umar, who shared a philosophy in which abstraction and the Arabic letter, were central to their approach. This was also to prove influential on artists such as Rafa Nasiri and Dia al-Azzawi. See Nada Shabout, "Shakir Hassan Al Said," in: *Archaic. The Pavilion of Iraq. 57th International Art Exhibition La Biennale di Venezia* (Naples: Mousse Publishing / Ruya Foundation, 2017), 65–6. See also Anneka Lenssen, Sarah Rogers and Nada Shabout, "Art and the Letter," in: *Modern Art and the Arab World: Primary Documents* (Durham: Duke University Press, 2018), 357–62. For Rafa al-Nasiri see Sabah al-Nasiri and May Muzaffar *Rafa al-Nasiri His life & Art* (Amman: The Arab Institute for Research and Publishing, 2010) and Sonja Mejcher-Atassi and May Muzaffar, eds., *Rafa Nasiri Artist Books* (Milan: Skira editore S.p.A, 2016).

6

http://www.roseissa.com/past%20 exhib/KUFA-walid/walid.html

7

Raad Mushatat's publications include *At Home and in Exile* (1986).

8

Writing as Samir al-Khalil, author of *The Monument Art, Vulgarity and Responsibility in Iraq* (London: André Deutch Ltd, 1991) and *The Republic of Fear* (Darby PA: Diane Publishing Co, 1989).

9

Kanan Makiya, Preface to *Dark Interludes* (2001).

1

I would like to thank Nat Muller and Walid Siti for inviting me to contribute to this beautiful book. This essay is based on a Skype conversation with Walid Siti on 15 February 2020. All the texts in quotation marks are from this interview.

2

Charles Tripp, *A History of Iraq*, 3rd ed. (Cambridge: Cambridge University Press, 2007), 162ff.

3

Tripp, *A History of Iraq*, 186.

4

Maysaloun Faraj, ed., *Strokes of Genius: Contemporary Iraqi Art* (London: Saqi books, 2001), 22. On the importance of Iraqi art at this time within the context of Arab art movements see "Considering Arab Art and Artists," in: Anneka Lenssen, Sarah Rogers and Nada Shabout, eds., *Modern Art and the Arab World: Primary Documents* (New York: The Museum of Modern Art, 2018), 170–173. There was a second art school in Baghdad at this time known as the Academy of Fine Arts.

Skylines, 2013. Inkjet print on paper.
210 × 330 cm.

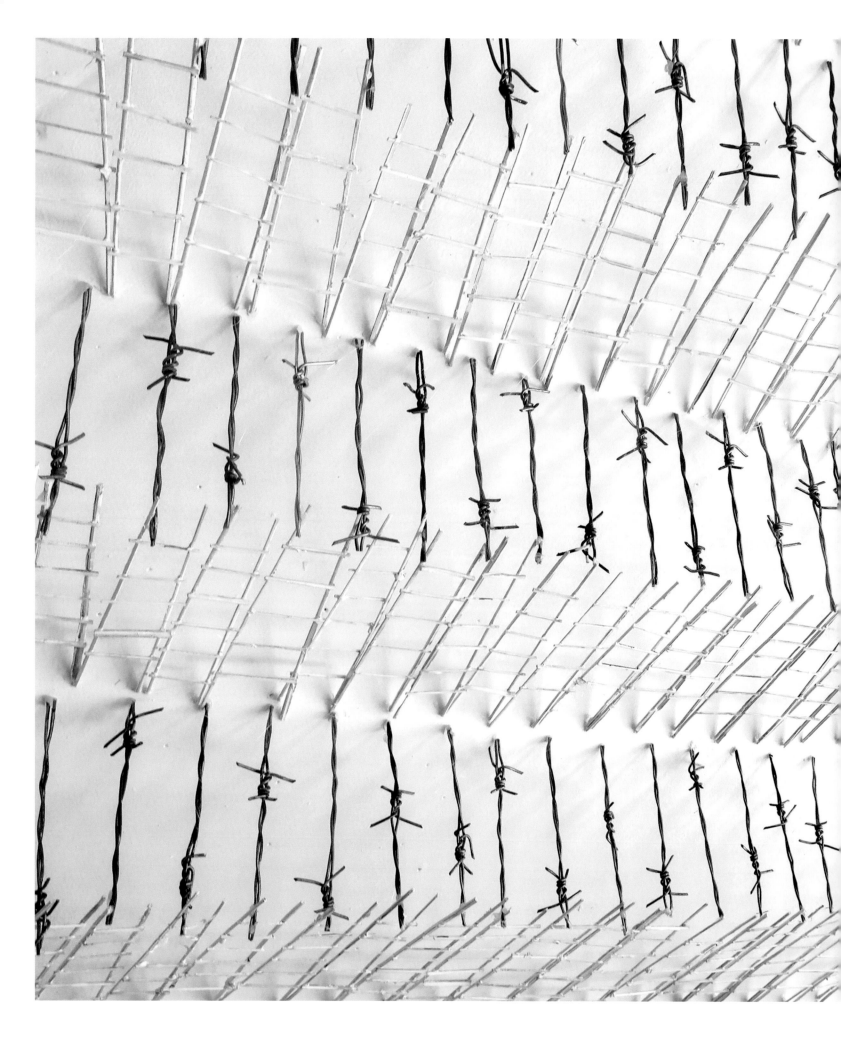

Rite of Passage, 2017. Wall-based installation. Barbed wire, straw and acrylic. 310 × 265 × 15 cm.
Solo exhibition *The Black Tower* at Zilberman Gallery, Berlin, 2017.

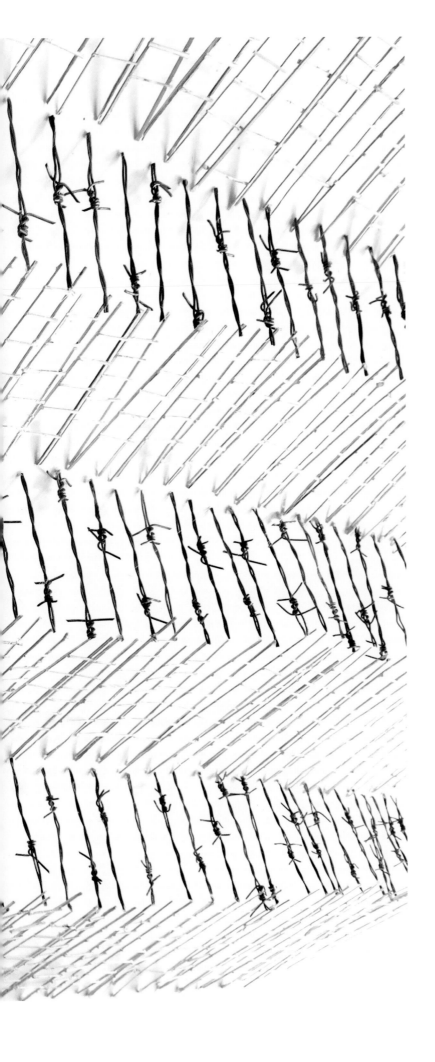

The Silver Lining, 2013. Wall-based installation, detail. Mylar mirror and barbed wire.
245 × 1500 × 30 cm. Solo exhibition *Crossing* at Amed Art Gallery, Diyarbakir, 2013.

Monument to the Ordinaries, 2015. Marble on board.
35 × 35 × 35 cm. Courtesy of Zilberman Gallery, Istanbul.
Photo credit: Kayhan Kaygusuz.

The Troubled Bear and the Palace, 2019. Video stills.
Photo credit: Salar Mudir and Mahamed Jori.

Ceremonies, 2016. Plastic figurines and straw. 40 × 40 × 40 cm.

Black Tower, 2016. Plastic figurines, paper, acrylic, plaster and twigs. 40 × 50 × 40 cm.

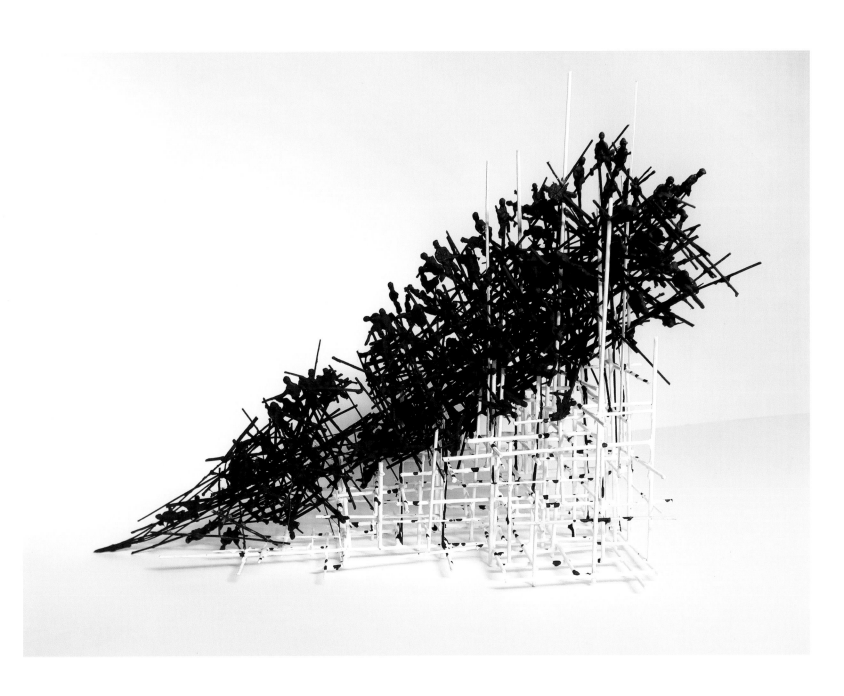

Fragile Permanence, 2016. Plastic figurines, straw and acrylic. 40 × 58 × 36 cm.

Imprints, 2016. Straw, plastic figurines, plaster and acrylic. 30 × 30 × 60 cm.

Wheel of Fortune, 2016. Barbed wire and plastic figurines on MDF. 80 × 80 × 15 cm.
Solo exhibition *The Black Tower* at Zilberman Gallery, Berlin, 2017.

War series, 1986. Crayon and ink on paper. 30 × 52 cm.

War series, 1986. Ink and acrylic on paper. 76 × 111 cm.   45

War series, 1988. Ink and acrylic on paper.
68.5 × 101 cm.

Moonlight, 1988. Woodcut on Japanese rice paper, AP. 49.5 × 63 cm.
Courtesy of the Trustees of the British Museum 1991, 0516,0.1. (Brooke Sewell Permanent Fund).

War series, 1986. Ink on paper. Both works 24 × 29 cm.

Dark Interludes, 2001. Number 1 and number 9 from a boxed set of 13 etchings on Somerset paper, numbered 12/50. 29.5 × 42 cm. Courtesy of the Trustees of the British Museum 2006, 0130,0.1-13 (Brooke Sewell Permanent Fund).

War series, 1986. Ink and crayon on paper. 29 × 24 cm.

War series, 1986. Ink and acrylic on paper. 29 × 16 cm.

Tormented Landscape series, 1989. Acrylic on paper. 35 × 45 cm.

Untitled, 2001. Mixed media on card. 33.5 × 47 cm.
Courtesy of the Trustees of the British Museum 2009, 6002.2.

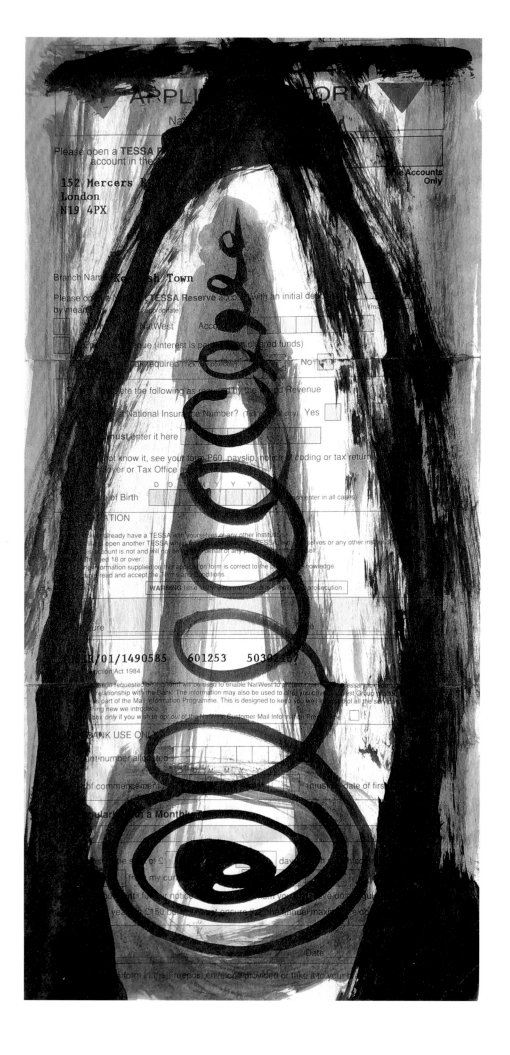

War series, 1986. Ink on paper. 30 × 15 cm.

War series, 1986. Ink, acrylic and collage on paper. 58 × 76 cm.

War series, 1987. Ink, crayon and acrylic on paper. 58 × 76 cm.

War series, 1986. Acrylic and ink on paper. 34 × 20 cm.

War series, 1987. Crayon and pencil on paper. 58 × 92 cm.

Tormented Landscape series, 1991. Ink and crayon paper. 20 × 29 cm.
Tormented Landscape series, 1991. Ink, pencil and crayon on paper. 15 × 21 cm.
Tormented Landscape series, 1993. Acrylic, ink and crayon on paper. 56 × 76 cm.

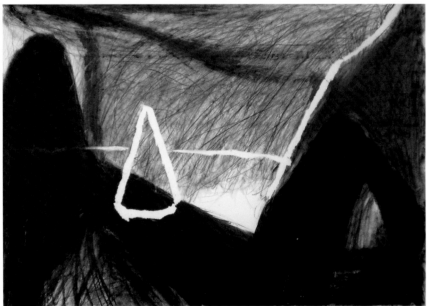

Tormented Landscape series, 1993. Acrylic and crayon on paper. 30 × 52 cm.
Tormented Landscape series, 1993. Crayon on paper. 56 × 76 cm.
Tormented Landscape series, 1991. Crayon and acrylic on paper. 56 × 76 cm.

Tormented Landscape series, 1991. Ink and crayon on paper. 17 × 24 cm.

Tormented Landscape series, 1991. Ink, pencil and crayon on paper. 18 × 23 cm.
Tormented Landscape series, 1991. Ink, pencil and crayon on paper. 16 × 20 cm.

Tormented Landscape series, 1991. Ink, pencil and crayon on paper. 20 × 18 cm.

Tormented Landscape series, 1991. Ink and crayon on paper. 30 × 21 cm.

Tormented Landscape series, 1991. Ink and crayon on paper. 15 × 20 cm.

Landscape + Architecture

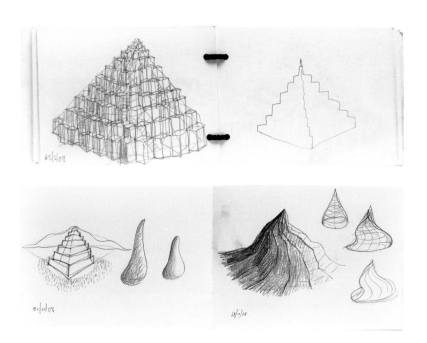

↑ Study for *Tower* series, 2008. Pencil on paper. 14 × 40 cm.
↑ Study for *Mountain* series, 2008. Pencil on paper. 14 × 40 cm.
→ Artist at work. Istanbul, 2015.

Walid Siti:
Landscape, History and War

Zainab Bahrani

Zainab Bahrani is the Edith
Porada Professor of Art History
and Archaeology at Columbia
University, New York. She is
the author of several books,
including *Rituals of War* (New
York: Zone Books, 2008) which
won the James Henry Breasted
Prize, and *The Infinite Image:
Art, Time and the Aesthetic
Dimension in Antiquity* (Reaktion
Books / University of Chicago
Press, 2014) which won the Lionel
Trilling Prize. She is also the
editor and co-author of several
other books written to accom-
pany exhibitions that she has
curated. Notable among them are
*Scramble for the Past: A Story of
Archaeology in the Ottoman Empire*
(Istanbul, 2011) and *Modernism
and Iraq* (New York, 2009). She
writes on topics ranging from
ancient art and archaeology to
contemporary art and Modernism in
the Middle East. She has written
extensively on the politics of
preservation and the destruction
of cultural heritage in Iraq
and Syria. Bahrani was born in
Baghdad, Iraq and educated in
Europe and the United States.
She is the recipient of numerous
fellowships and awards for her
research including awards from
the Getty Foundation, the Mellon
Foundation and a 2003 Guggenheim
award. She currently directs a
field project in Iraq and Turkey,
Mapping Mesopotamian Monuments.

The landscape of antiquity, the archaeological earth that holds the past and upon which so many ancient mounds and structures are visible today, has had a significant impact on the shaping of the artists of the Modern and Contemporary era in Iraq. An awareness of the Meso-potamian past, resulting from early twentieth-century archaeological research and exploration played a role here, certainly in the development of the arts. This aware-ness of the ancient past became an area of much thought in the work of artists from across Iraq. But besides the new archaeological developments, it was also the visual impact of the impressive monuments themselves, their continuing and steadfast presence. These monuments still stand after many centuries, visible to the viewer in the diverse natural landscapes of the region. This an-cient Mesopotamian land, from the rugged highlands of Kurdistan to the picturesque marshes of the Iraqi south, the place where Sumerian art and culture first emerged in the fourth millennium BC, were constantly referenced by the twentieth-century Pioneers Group (al Ruwad) and the Baghdad School of Modernism in a conscious and deliberate way. These artists who flourished in the 1940s through the 1960s, referred to this reception of the past and historical heritage as Istilham al Turath, a return to the past in order to find the present, to receive inspiration from it. In the words of Jewad Salim, the leading artist of the Modernist movement in Iraq whose works have had the greatest influence on both modern and contemporary art, this is 'an explosive continuation of the past' rather than a revival.[1] Walid Siti, an artist of a generation that was born into this world takes this historical landscape, with its monuments and its history into his works as a central theme. Yet, having come after the revolutionary Modernist moment of mid-twentieth-century Iraq when artists were struggling to express liberation from British occupation and a desire for nationhood, Siti's art moves from there into another direction, and reflects another historical experience of place that came afterwards. At the same time as referencing the ancient historical land-scape of his country with its iconic monuments, he also takes its recent history of violence and its wounds and forges them all into a statement of identity. Yet, the iden-tity that we see in his work does not seem to be either nationalist or based in ethnicity. It is not celebratory or prideful, despite its references to the past. Instead, what we see is a complexity of identity in his work, and an art that also often brings to mind the troubled experience of exile and displacement, despite a strong link to the land. Displacement, we might observe, is a removal from place, a disconnection that is never fixed and with which one must constantly contend.

↗ Artist in his London studio, 2005.
↑ Study for *Precious Stones* series, 1997. Pen on paper. 18 × 40 cm.
↑ Study for *Tower* series, 1997. Pen on paper. 18 × 40 cm.

The work titled <u>Phantom Land</u> is a 2017 installation, as the earlier work <u>A Wasteland</u> (2016), they are made of wooden board with grout and acrylic shaped into an unidentifiable map in each case. These works seem not to be a reference to a real place. Appearing to be a bird's eye view, or perhaps an aerial view of a mapped region that one ought to recognise as militarised target, the artist uses the visual idioms of a scientific gaze while at the same time he shakes up that certainty of a real, mapped site. At first glance, the viewer wonders what and where it is. <u>A Wasteland</u>, charcoal black, gives the impression of scorched earth and perhaps petroleum. It seems like a satellite view, tilted and compartmentalised, as if a scientifically-based image of a real location, yet it is not there. Siti's <u>Phantom Land</u>, a white composition shown directly on the floor, blending into the exhibition floor, is likewise not to be easily located. It is a no man's land, similar to the postmodern non-place of migration and displacement, of alienation. On the other hand, the militarized distant perspective also suggests a place that has been and remains today, a surreal target in the western view; a territory of warfare that is both there and not there, as the statement at the beginning of stories, such as those of a <u>One Thousand and One Nights</u> might say, 'there was and there wasn't' such a place. Thus <u>Tormented Landscape</u> of 1991–93, a series of ink, pencil and crayon works on paper created at the time of the First Gulf War (1990–91) and subsequent uprisings of the population in both Kurdistan and the south of Iraq that were brutally put down by the Saddam Hussein regime, and his 1980s <u>War</u> series, ink and acrylic on paper, are historical landscapes with iconic monuments darkened by the fog and smoke of war. We see the collapsing spiral minaret of Samarra in central Iraq and a sculptural head resembling a Sumerian statue fallen on its side, we see a hill that seems to be an archaeological <u>tell</u> (an artificial mound accumulated through time) referencing the antiquity of the landscape with a similar sculpted head upon it, the dark flag and fog of war surround all these mournful scenes that have come to define the land and the experience of its people.

In the video work titled, <u>The Troubled Bear and the Palace</u> (2019), Siti shows us the former palace of Saddam Hussein built in 1989, the ruins of which remains atop the Gara Mountain close to the border of Iraqi Kurdistan and Turkey. There, a televised ceremony took place in 2018 in which two bears were released to symbolise the overthrow of this oppressive regime and liberation from it. Although meant to convey freedom for these beasts, the release is disturbing for the viewer. The bears seem to have lost the dignity required to proceed and stumble away from their cages. Consequently, the bears struggled to survive because they had been caged for their entire existence. One bear seems to have disappeared into the wilderness and probably does not survive, while the second bear is living in distress in the palace ruin as if unable to move on from its own imprisonment. The video quotes from the <u>Epic of Gilgamesh</u> (the world's earliest epic tale dating to the third millennium BC and first written in Sumerian in southern Iraq) about the nature of absolute kingship, a type of rule that is embodied in this location where the regime had total surveillance of the land. The lines from the epic also describe the boundary between life and death and existence in the netherworld at the same time that we view the last bear trapped by its own timidity within the hellscape of this ruined palace. In that sense the ceremony of freedom and the troubled bear, become a sign of the continuing long-term ramifications of oppression and violence still to be seen in the landscape of Kurdistan and indeed, across Iraq.

Landscapes can carry the iconic signs of a rich historical past, but they can conversely be a charged place for ethno-nationalisms, for violent regimes and for corruption associated with capitalist development, all of which plague the region today. Here and elsewhere in earlier works, an architectonic precision is used to convey a place that is there and not there. These structures and landscapes are exacting representations, yet they are cryptic and enigmatic. Like the images and objects of Surrealism they provoke and disturb the imagination. Siti's landscapes are uncanny and disturbing, fraught with images of destruction, collapse, war, but also deeply anchored in a historical sense of place that constantly carries a trace of mourning and loss within it.

One such uncanny disturbing object is <u>Wheel of Fortune</u> (2016). A work composed of barbed wire and plastic figures of soldiers; it is an object that unsettles the viewer. The wheel of twisted and barbed wire contains figures of people trapped and falling, both within it and out of it. This is the cog, the mechanism of the machinery of war and violence that is the fate of this region, Iraqi Kurdistan, an area that suffered unspeakable attacks by the former regime, and Iraq in general, a land devastated by wars that continue today as I write this essay at the start of 2020. Although the barbed wire frames and forms the image of fate here in a particularly significant way, barbed wire and fences appear elsewhere in Siti's work. The <u>Wheel of Fortune</u> where fate is a barbed wheel that entraps and hurls forward, is paralleled by mountain images where the mountain also reappears as a barbed grid that criss-crosses the land. Elusive Mountain (2018) is a barbed wire and aluminium wire structure, a mountain that cannot be scaled. These are violent objects of war, but they are also objects of separation and division. In Rite of Passage (2016), a work of barbed wire, straw and acrylic, rows of wires are the rite that must be passed, as for displaced peoples, there is no right of movement. Likewise, within Iraq, including Iraqi Kurdistan, stopping at checkpoints and encountering barbed wire fences have become the common lived experience of people, turning the landscape into a terrain of war and division. These boundaries exist at approaches to cities, as well as within cities and in the countryside, subdividing areas and controlling the movement of the population in their daily lives. At the same time, one sees internally displaced people living in barbed wire encampments within their very own country.

Mountains and towers are main themes of Siti's works. The Malwiya minaret, part of the grand mosque of Samarra built in the ninth century AD when the Abbasid capital moved from Baghdad to Samarra, figures prominently through the decades of his representations. In his youth Siti visited the Malwiya minaret and was impressed by this experience, and he has returned there in more recent years, climbing the winding steps of the tower for the first time. This ascent involves a movement upwards in a spiral that gives a vast vision of the Mesopotamian landscape around it, and it is a process of ritual ascent that plays on the sense of the sublime by means of its awe-inspiring, open elevation. Climbing the Malwiya is a process that has an effect similar to scaling a steep mountainside.

As an architectural structure, the Samarra spiral minaret echoes the Ziggurat of Ur and the Tower of Babel in shape. Early travellers from Europe in fact confused it with the legendary tower of Babylon that they knew from Biblical accounts. It was illustrated in European manuscripts and in paintings such as Pieter Brueghel's The Tower of Babel now in Vienna. The Malwiya in Siti's art is also like the Ziggurats of Mesopotamia, the stepped temple towers that were built through thousands of years of Mesopotamian antiquity. The ziggurat was an axis mundi, and so the Malwiya seems to be in its reappearances. It is worth noting that Siti derives images from the past, but they are not past, they are present in the landscape that he knows. Thus towers and landscapes and the divine converge, in the same way that they did in the Mesopotamian imagination. The ancient name of the temple of Babylon is Etemenanki which means 'the

bond of the foundation of heaven and earth.' This too appears in the works on paper and is identified as such in the Tower series sketchbook (2008) with Amran written below, the name of a tell, an artificial mound in Babil that resulted from thousands of years of life on this site. As many other ancient and legendary sites here, they are impressive and impactful in their continuity of the past. The screen of images we see in Wall Intervention Installation exhibited at the Baghdad Mon Amour exhibition in Paris in 2018 brings together this interconnected iconography of towers, ziggurats, spiral minarets and steps, ladders and mountains, and ritual sites of circumambulation. These works of ink and crayon on paper are affixed to a larger board creating a wall, a site of inter-referentiality that echoes across time and space.

Walid Siti was born in Dohuk, a city surrounded by mountains that are brown and grey by the end of the summer but covered in a deep emerald green foliage in the months of spring. Just outside this city, Assyrian rock reliefs can be seen from the side of the road, carved into the cliffs. The relationship of the ancient past of Mesopotamia and the land is more than a metaphor here; it is a visible and tangible presence of the past literally carved into the terrain. It is the character of the landscape and it can ignite the imagination; it is a constant reminder of the historical past that continues into our own time. Walid Siti is also an exiled artist. Exile is a thing in itself to consider, alongside any other aspect of the interrogation of identity, there is the state of being in exile which is a state of constant displacement. Siti was granted asylum in the United Kingdom in 1984. But he has recently been refused a visa to attend an exhibition of his own work as part of a group show for Kurdish artists called Speaking Across Mountains that opened in Washington D.C. in December 2019. An Iraqi, Kurdish or not, in today's world is generally treated with suspicion, and Siti is no exception.

Another theme in the more recent works is the way in which development in Iraqi Kurdistan is fast destroying the stunning natural landscape and historical character of the environment but also of cities such as Erbil, one of the oldest continuously inhabited sites in the world, where settlement goes back to the Neolithic period, and the name of which is recorded as Erbil / Arbil already in the third millennium BC cuneiform texts. The Erbil citadel, rising upon an ancient artificial mound or tell in the ancient texts, is being renovated and turned into a tourist site. The lower town below, an old city with similar houses and khans (inns) directly adjacent to the Qaissariyeh / Bazaar of Erbil was emptied of its population recently with the idea of renovation. However, the historical brickwork houses are neglected and left to collapse, most likely in order to allow development firms to build high-rises next to the ancient citadel in their place. History and local identity are thus sold out to transnational interests. In Chasing the Utopia (2011), Siti raises these concerns of the construction boom in Erbil that mirrors the new cities of the United Arab Emirates such as Dubai. Likewise, in Beauty Spot, shown at the 2011 Iraqi Pavilion in Venice, Wounded Water, we see the privatisation and monetisation of the Gali Ali Beg waterfalls. The work represents a 5000 dinar note with a flowing waterfall at its centre. This is a tourist site northeast of Erbil where the government hired a private company to pump water into the falls for tourism and water sports, while there is a water crisis and large scale poverty in a country that is wealthy enough to provide for its own people, but does not do so.

Black, white and earthen tones are the colours that we see throughout the works. They are limited, sombre and dark. Siti's works are melancholic, but these are also the colours of draftsmanship, architectural sketching and exactitude as if to lay out the evidence of a place and the echoes of its history. He maps and charts a landscape that is punctuated with iconic historical monuments and deep history, yet also a landscape tormented by violence, warfare and discord, thus he is an artist for our own time.

1
See Zainab Bahrani and Nada Shabout, *Modernism and Iraq* (New York: The Wallach Art Gallery, 2009), 11-22. See also the 1951 Manifesto of the Baghdad Group for Modern Art and the 'Renewal of Art' by Jewad Salim in Anneka Lenssen, Sarah Rogers and Nada Shabout, eds., *Modern Art in the Arab World: Primary Documents* (New York: The Museum of Modern Art, 2018), 150-2.

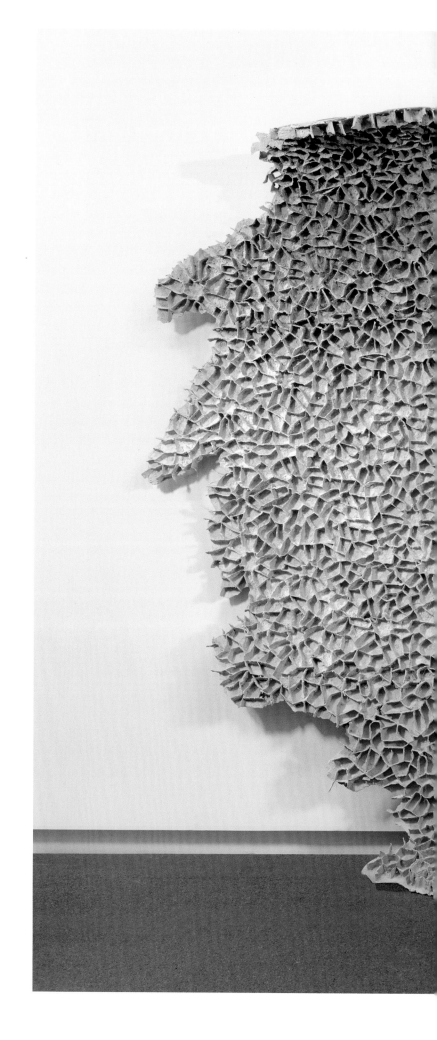

Floodland, 2017. Grey board, grout, plaster and acrylic
on plywood. 250 × 360 × 90 cm. Group exhibition
Age of Terror at The Imperial War Museum, London, 2017.
Courtesy of the Imperial War Museum.

Installation view *Beauty Spot*, 2011. C-print on board with looped video. 220 × 440 cm.
The Iraqi Pavilion exhibition *Wounded Water* at the 54th International Venice Biennale, 2011.
Courtesy of Sala 1 International Centre for Contemporary Art.

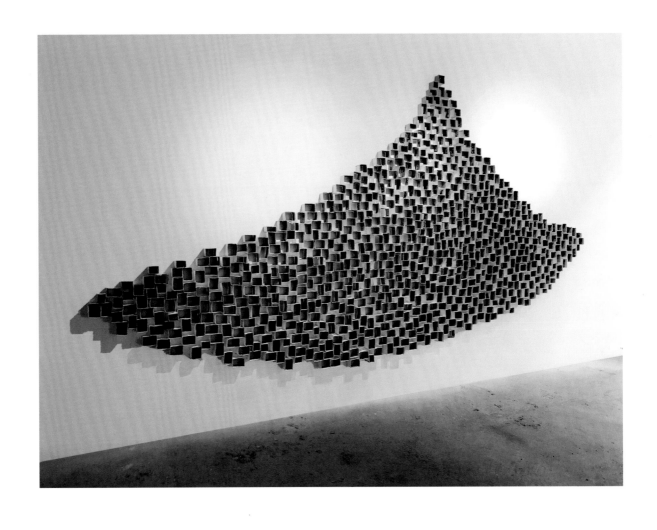

Stone Tales, 2018. Hard paper, acrylic, newspaper offcuts, and glue. 340 × 600 × 10 cm.
Group exhibition *Impossible to Find* at Latitude Gallery Art Space, Yerevan, 2019.

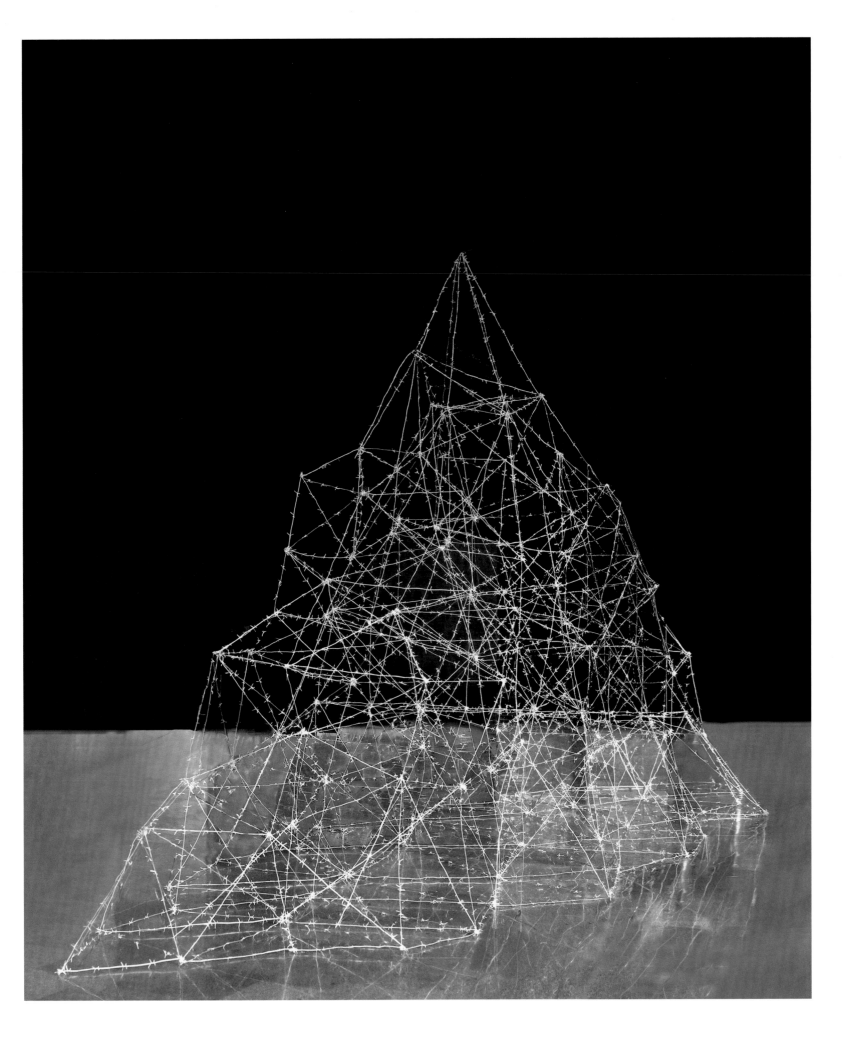

Elusive Mountain, 2018. Barbed wire and thin aluminium wire. 400 × 800 × 300 cm.
Group exhibition *International Contemporary Art Exhibition*, Yerevan, 2018.

One Way Up, 2016. Plastic figurines and straw. 40 × 40 × 40 cm.

Untitled, 2019. Twigs, plaster and acrylic. 50 × 50 × 50 cm.

The Tower, 2015. Site-specific installation. Wood and MDF board. 500 × 500 × 700 cm.
Art Istanbul International, Istanbul, 2015.

Chasing the Utopia, 2011. Straw and acrylic on MDF board. 40 × 40 × 40 cm.

Constructing Mountain, 2012. Straw, clay and acrylic paint on MDF board. 40 × 40 × 40 cm.

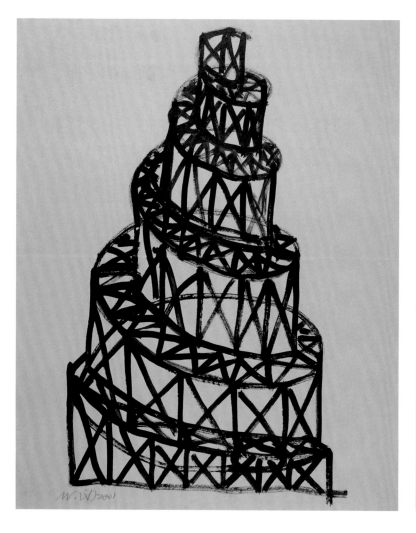 

Minaret of Samarra, Tower series, 2001. Ink on paper. 55 × 40 cm.
Untitled, Tower series, 2001. Ink on paper. 55 × 40 cm.

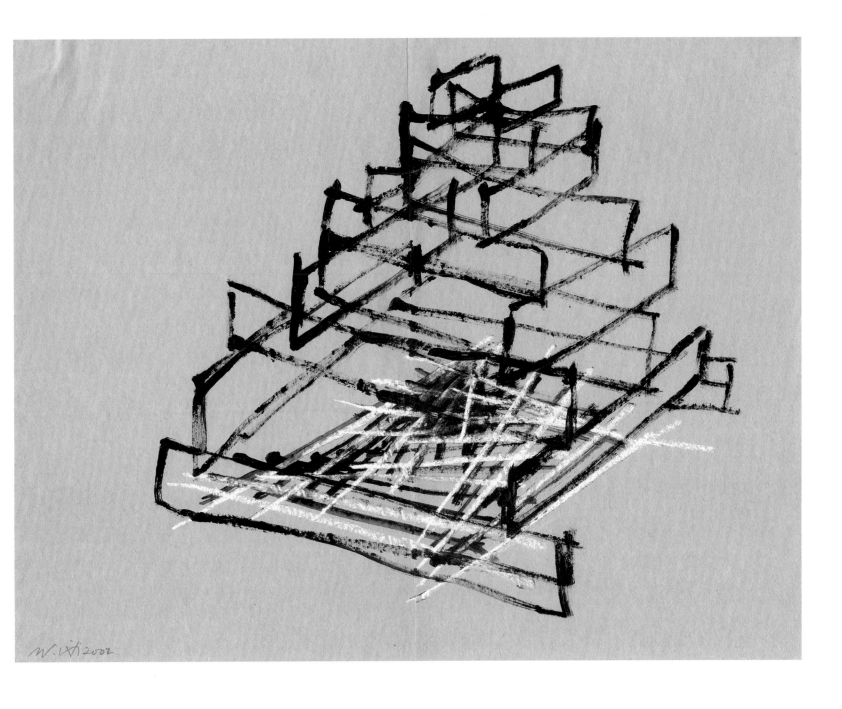

Ziggurat, Tower series, 2001. Acrylic and crayon on paper. 40 × 55 cm.

Tower series, 2014. Pastel on paper. 42 × 28 cm.

Sphere, 2001. Acrylic and crayon on paper. 33 × 44 cm.

Pyramid, Tower series, 2001. Acrylic and ink on paper. 40 × 55 cm.

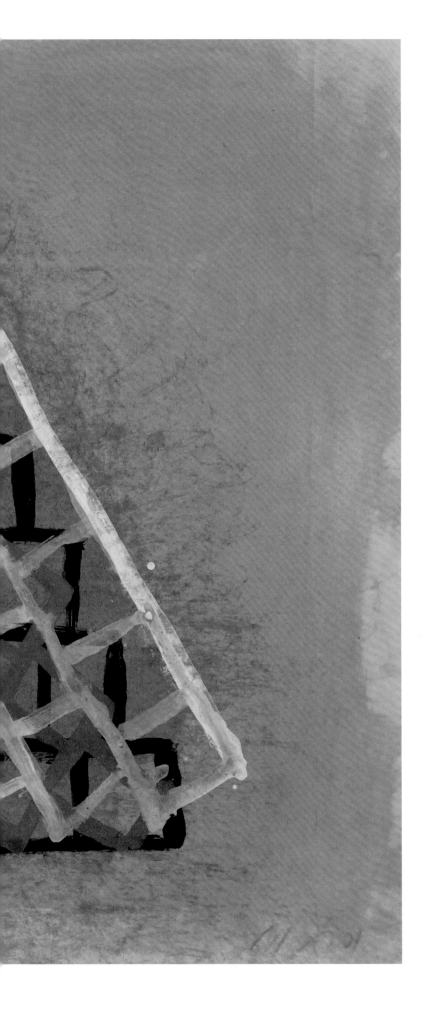

Untitled, 2001. Charcoal and white chalk on brown paper. 32.5 × 32 cm.
Courtesy of the Trustees of the British Museum 2009, 6002.1.

Tower series, 2016. Acrylic on paper. All sketches 42 × 28 cm.

Tower series, 2013. Acrylic and pastel on paper. 82 × 59 cm.

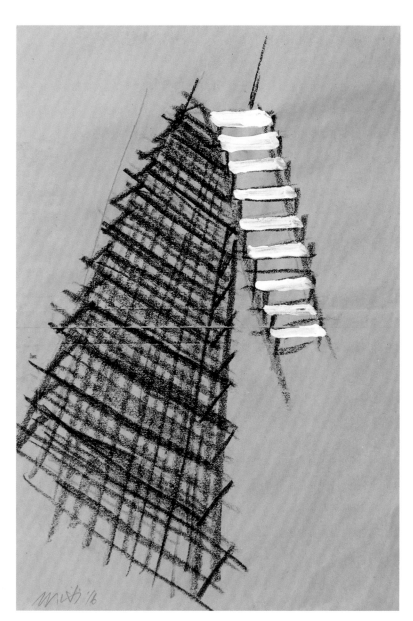

Tower series, 2016. Acrylic and pastel on paper. All sketches 42 × 28 cm.

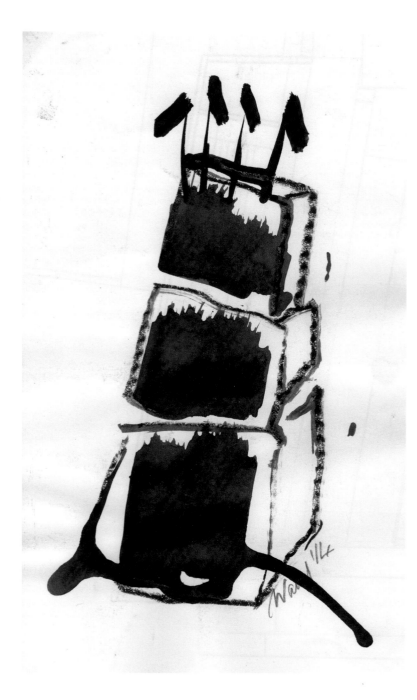

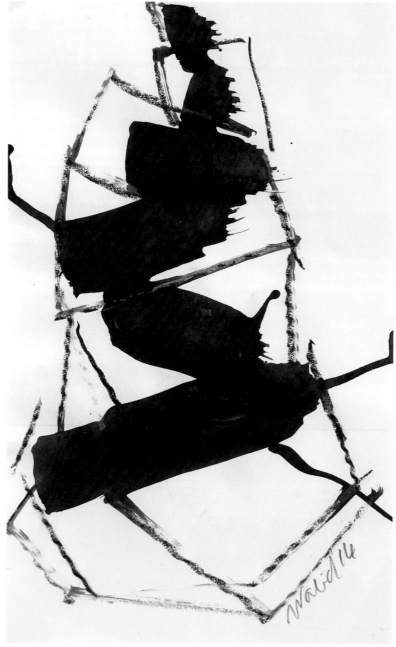

Tower series, 2016. Acrylic and pastel on paper. Both sketches 42 × 28 cm.

 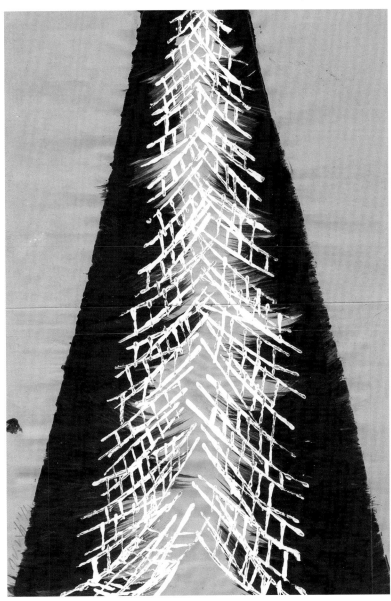

Tower series, 2012. Acrylic on paper. 50 × 60 cm.
Tower series, 2016. Acrylic on paper. 42 × 28 cm.

Tower series, 2013. Acrylic and graphite. 56 × 76 cm.

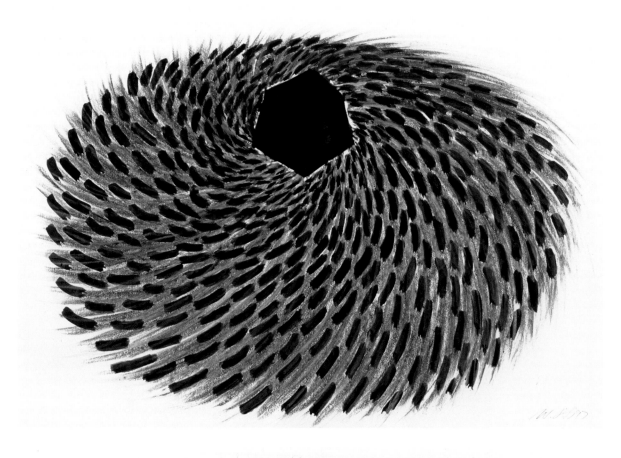

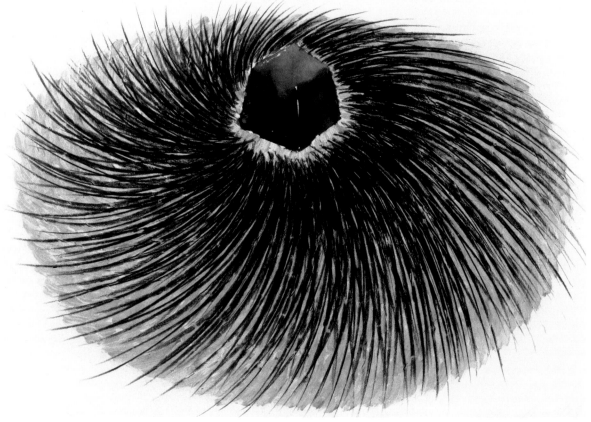

Precious Stones series, 1997. Ink and crayon on paper. 56 × 76 cm.
Precious Stones series, 1997. Ink, acrylic and crayon on paper. 56 × 76 cm.

Precious Stones series, 1997. Monotype on paper. 56 × 76 cm.
Precious Stones series, 1997. Pastel on paper. 56 × 76 cm.

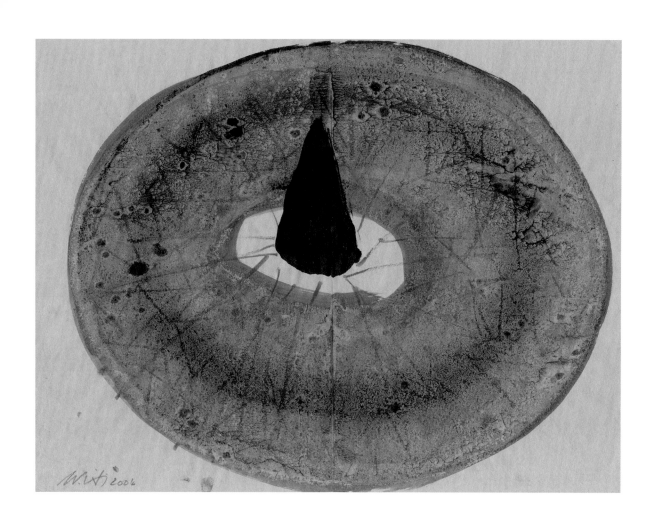

Precious Stones series, 2004. Monoprint on paper. 31 × 42 cm.

Precious Stones series, 1997. Ink, acrylic and crayon on paper. 56 × 76 cm.

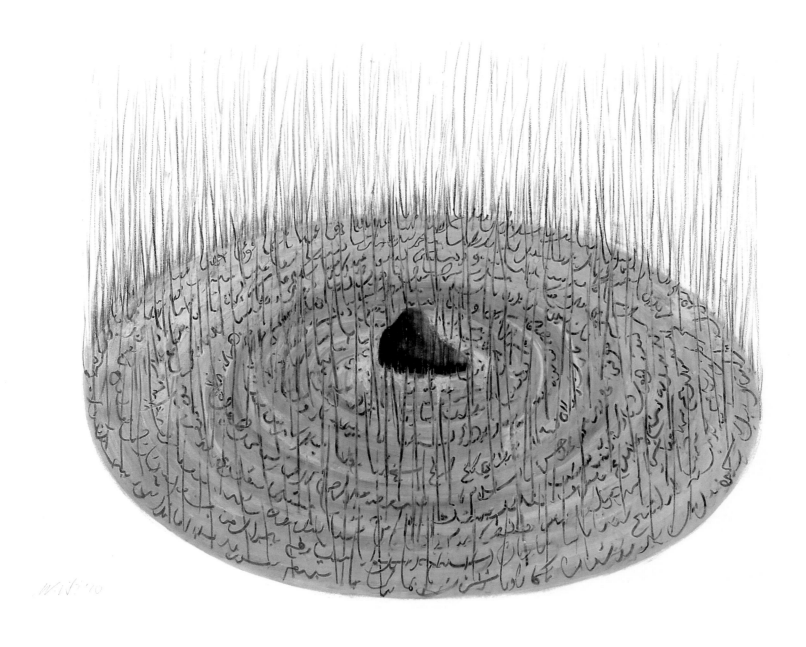

Precious Stones series, 2010. Acrylic and graphite on paper. 77 × 100 cm.

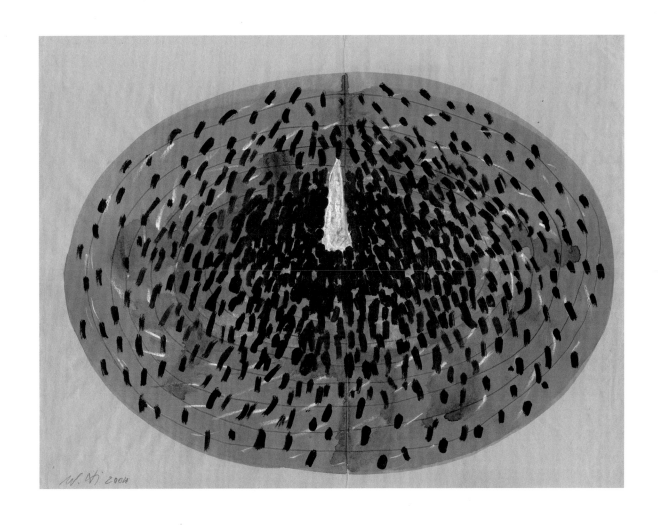

Precious Stones series, 2004. Acrylic, crayon and graphite on paper. 31 × 42 cm.

Precious Stones series, 1997. Ink, acrylic and crayon on paper. 56 × 76 cm.

Mountains series, 2008. Acrylic, pastel and graphite on paper. 56 × 76 cm.

Mountains series, 2008. Acrylic and graphite on paper. 34 × 24 cm.

Mountains series, 2009. Monotype on paper. 56 × 76 cm.

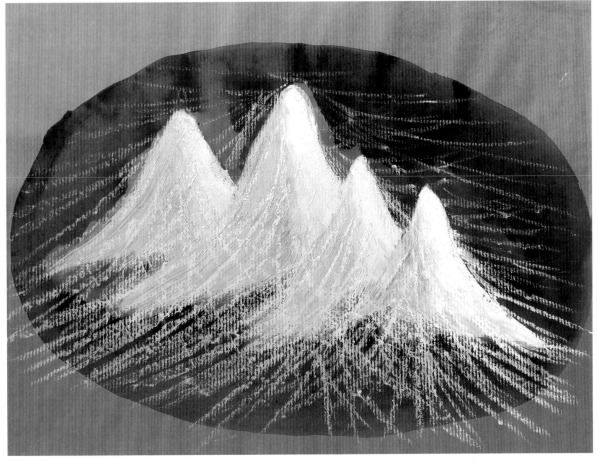

Mountains series, 2014. Acrylic and crayon on paper. 28 × 38 cm.

Mountains series, 2010. Acrylic, crayon and graphite on paper. 56 × 76 cm.

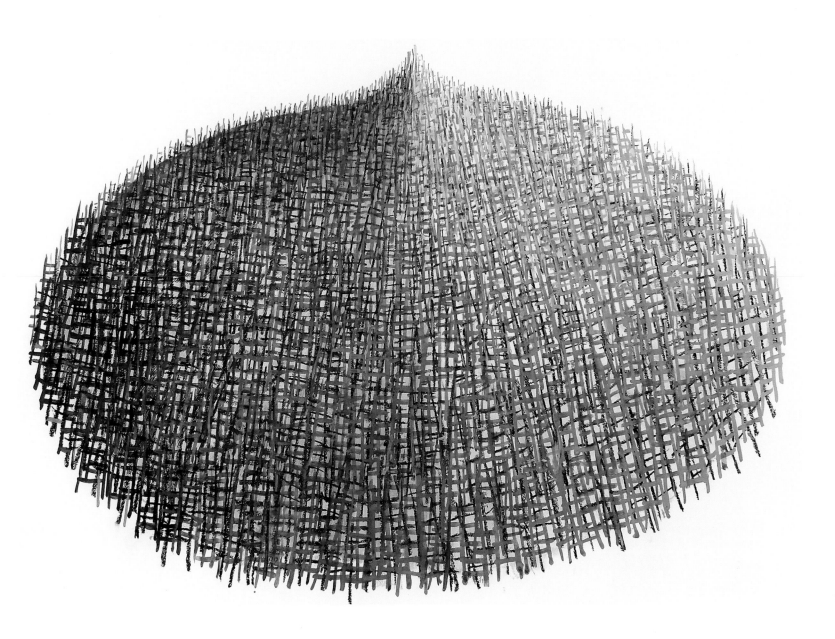

Mountains series, 2012. Acrylic and crayon on paper. 56 × 76 cm.

Mountains series, 2010. Acrylic and crayon on paper.
56 × 76 cm.

Traces, 2013. Acrylic and pastel on paper. 25 × 35 cm.

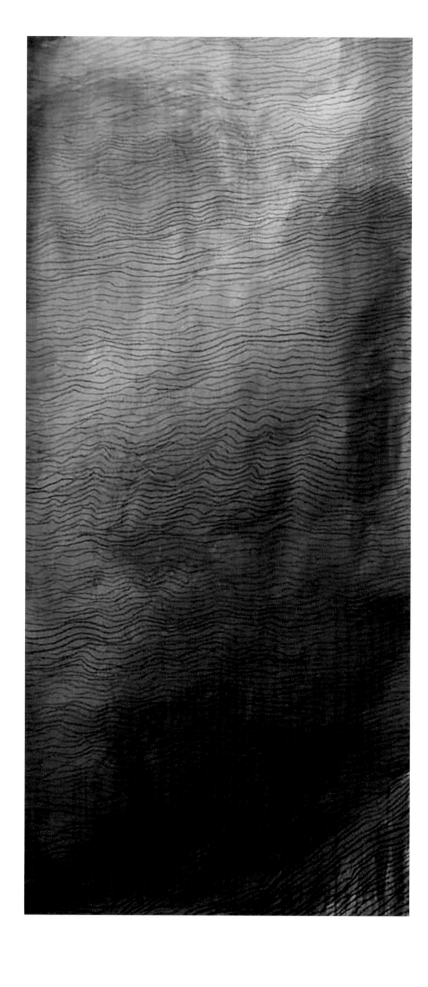

Paths, 2013. Acrylic and crayon on paper.
217 × 300 cm.

The White Peak, 2011. Acrylic on paper. 56 × 76 cm.   130

131

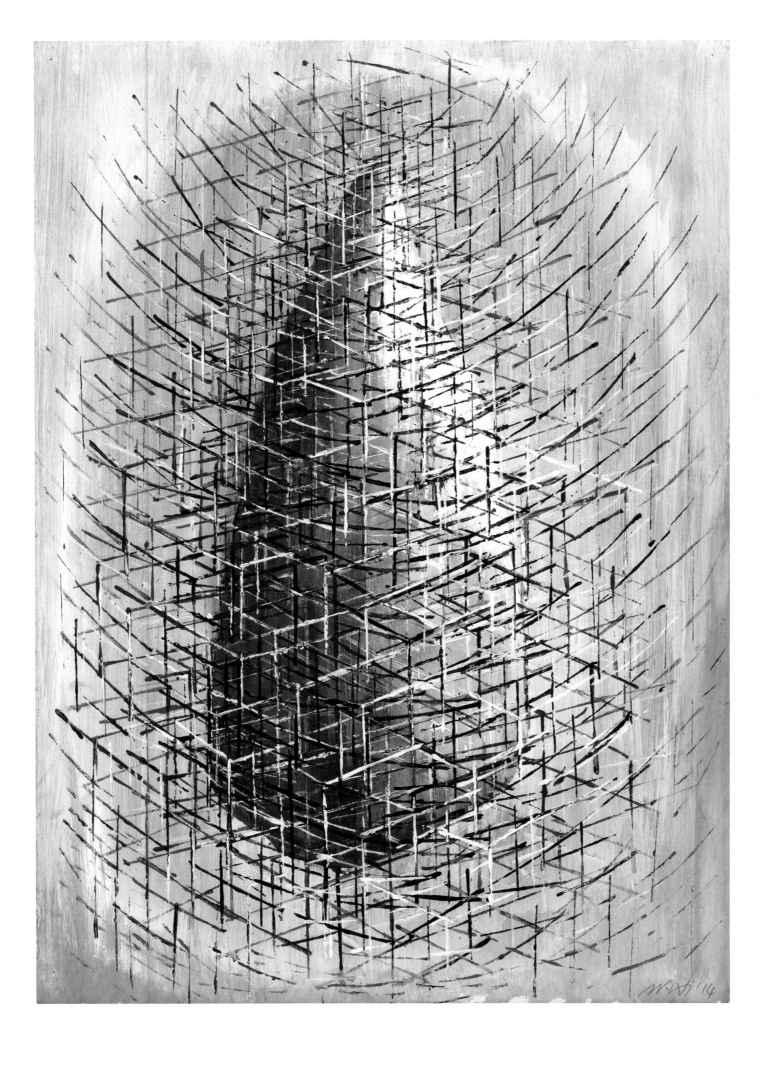

The Lonely Rock, Mountains series, 2014. Acrylic on paper. 76 × 56 cm.

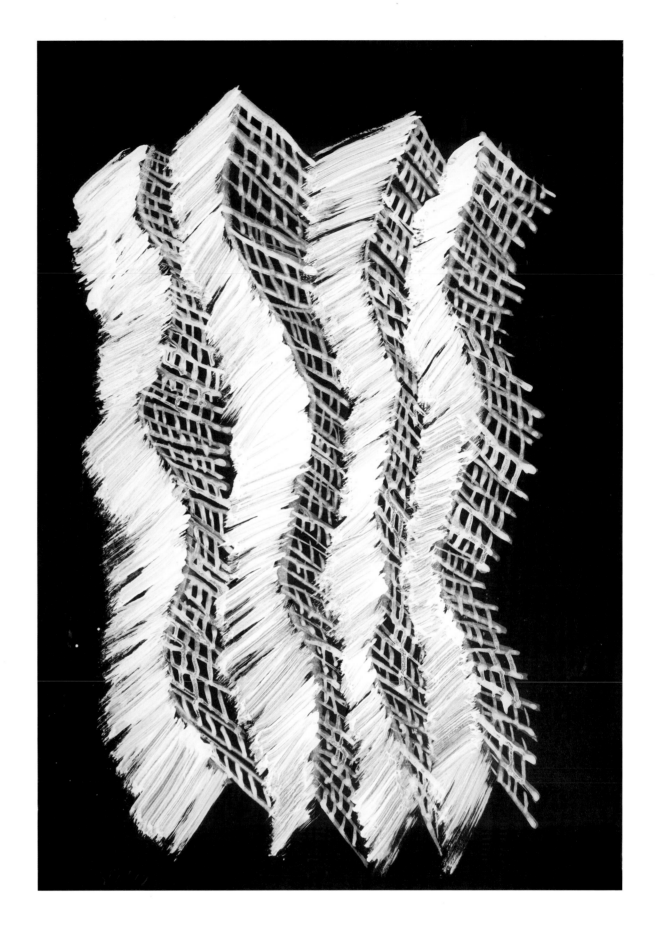

String, Mountains series, 2017. Acrylic on paper. 55 × 38 cm.

Mountains series, 2010. Acrylic on canvas.
146 × 280 cm.

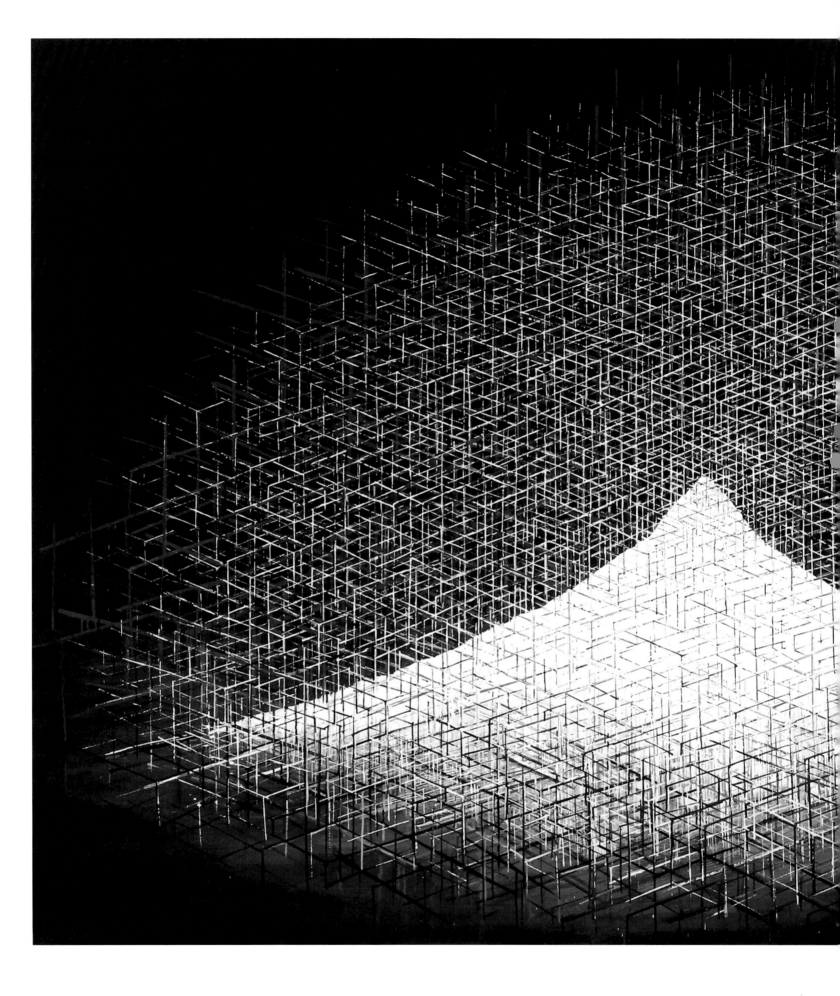

Monument to a Forgotten Story, 2013. Acrylic on canvas. 185 × 280 cm.
Photo credit: Alex Maguire.

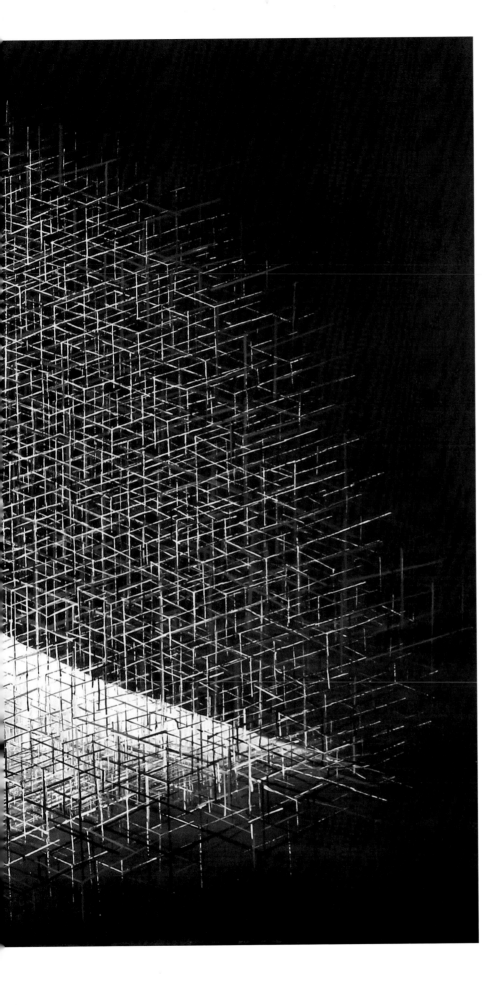

A Poem to Mountain at the Edge of the World, 2019. Acrylic on MDF.
163 × 300 × 7 cm. Group exhibition *Speaking Across Mountains*
at the Middle East Institute, Washington D.C., 2019.

Mountains series, 2011. Acrylic and graphite on paper. Both works 80 × 60 cm.

Belonging
+
Exile

↑ The artist at work in London, 2016. Photo credit: Sheenwar Siti.
→ Sketch for *Anatomy of Climbing*, 2013. Graphite on paper. 29 × 41 cm.
→ Study from sketchbook, 1998. Ink on paper. 14 × 38 cm.

Tracing Constellations:
Belonging and Exile in the Practice of Walid Siti

Sarah Johnson

Sarah Johnson is the curator for
the Middle East and North Africa
collections at the National
Museum of World Cultures in
the Netherlands. Her doctoral
dissertation focused on the Iraqi
artist Hafidh Druby (1914-1991)
and alternative aesthetic moder-
nities in the Middle East. She
won the Rhonda A. Saad Prize in
2017 for her doctoral research on
the links between archaeology and
modernity in Iraq. Previously,
she was a curator of Islamic
collections at the British Museum
in London, where she worked on
the modern and contemporary
collections from the Middle East
and assisted with the curation of
the inaugural exhibition at the
King Abdulaziz Center for World
Culture in Dhahran, Saudi Arabia.
She was also a researcher for the
Middle East collections at the
Freer and Sackler Galleries in
Washington D.C. She has worked
in several artists' studios
and contributed to Artforum.
Her current projects include
an article on soldier-artists
stationed in Baghdad during WWII
and an exhibition on the links
between ethnography and modern
aesthetics in North Africa.

The oft-exiled Iraqi poet Abdul Wahab al-Bayati (1926–1999) wrote in his poem The Wound in 1961:

> Whenever you come back from exile
> Your eyes get focused on the old wound …
> Whenever you come back, you trace the wound
> in the same images.[1]

It was only when Walid Siti was exiled to London in 1984 at the age of thirty that his work began to fixate on a set group of forms connected to the Iraqi landscape – mount Zawa in Kurdistan, the ancient ziggurat towers, the ladder of a mudbrick house, the arch, and most persistently, the Malwiya minaret in Samarra. Siti did not climb the imposing and unique spiral minaret, which towers over the pockmarked ruin of a ninth-century early Islamic capital 78 miles north of Baghdad, until 2019. For most of his youth, he saw it from a distance on the bus back and forth from his home in Duhok to his studies at the Institute of Fine Arts in Baghdad because he was too poor to afford to get off the bus. Yet, the Malwiya appears in Siti's first sketches in London – frantic, almost apocalyptic, landscapes of broad overlapping brushstrokes, done on bits of newspaper, phone bills, or any scrap paper he could find with his limited finances. Gradually, his group of core topographic forms became the centre of more stayed compositions in which the structures themselves, such as the spiral of the minaret, informed the lines and movement of the sketch, painting or sculpture.

Siti refers to these repeating images in his work as 'icons.' Similar to religious icons, Siti finds power in these forms through their continual reworking and renewal in his practice. With a scientific methodology, he studies these forms through hundreds of sketches, leading to a painting or sculpture, which pars down the form to its geometric elements, as Siti puts it 'to get to the core of the idea.' Throughout painting, print, sculpture, and sketch, he builds these images in many different media and dissects them from various angles. In a corner of his studio, two cross-sections of the Malwiya made of cardboard boxes, each playing with varying scales and materialities, hang at eye level. In another corner, the spiral form is even imagined in photoshop, rising from a photograph of an unfinished concrete building.

But just as icons hold power in the consistency of the image, they can also be elusive, promising belonging and fulfilment without ever providing it. Throughout Siti's practice, his topographic leitmotifs are often obfuscated,

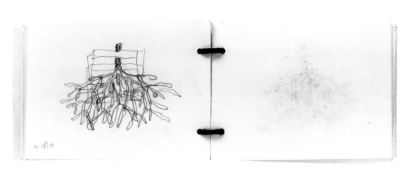

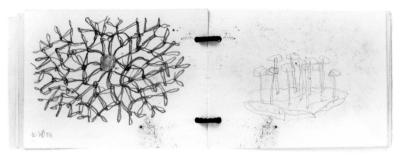

↑ Study for *Family Ties* series, 2004. Pencil on paper. 14 × 38 cm.
→ Artist working on the model *Tower*. Istanbul, 2015.

rupturing or disintegrating through the very repetition of their own form. In his painting series <u>Dialogue of Towers</u> (2013), the bricks of the Malwiya seem to multiply like a digital virus into infinite rectangular prisms, whose litany blurs the spiral form of the central image. In the third painting of the series, a tower of white ladders stands out starkly from a pitch-black background. Yet around its edges, ladders fade away in gradients of grey and black, at once building blocks and ephemeral forms that could collapse the tower through the simple gradation of greyscale.

In fact, in much of Siti's work, it is his forms that build from and surround the central geographic articulations which structure the composition. Siti's <u>Family Ties</u> series (2004) began with a group of sketches in which he studied the form of a tree upside down, with the branches spreading across the page in a web of interlocking lines. As the series progressed, these branches became increasingly abstracted into a plexus of nodes with connecting lines – simple and powerful representations of a network. In a few of the paintings from this series, the Malwiya or a more ambiguous tower appear in the centre, but it is the network, the web of dots and lines, that dominates the composition. In an apogee of this study, his series <u>A Perfect Formation</u> (2013), he replaces the usual topographic form at the centre with an empty hole surrounded by a web of threads wrapped around nails. As his work since has proved, this series was not a final annihilation of the geographic form but an experimentation with such a prospect – with the possibility that a network could exist without geographic markers. Yet topographies persist in his practice as both centripetal and centrifugal forces.

It is this personal negotiation between abstraction and geographical specificity and between topography and network that is at the heart of Siti's practice's relationship with belonging and exile, beyond his geographical peregrinations first from his home in Duhok in Kurdistan to Baghdad in 1971 at the age of seventeen, then from Baghdad to Ljubljana in 1976, and finally to London in 1984. It was not the ancient towers of the Iraqi landscape – the Malwiya minaret or the arch of Ctesiphon – that created for Siti a feeling of belonging as a Kurdish art student in Baghdad. Instead, it was the network of students who surrounded him. Despite their regional diversity from Kurdistan in the north to Basra in the south, they came together through their left-leaning politics and their desire to move beyond what they saw as the conservative art methods of their teachers.

In 1970s Baghdad, many artists and artist groups promoted a focus on realism and suppression of individuality in art in solidarity with global leftist and postcolonial movements. Rafa al-Nasiri, Siti's teacher, wrote in a manifesto in 1969 along with other prominent artists, such as Dia al-Azzawi, for their group <u>New Vision</u>: 'an artist grounds his justification for human existence in nature … making art not as a means of seclusion in individual existence or immersion in one's private world, but rather a vision directed to the world.'[2] For many, the biggest enemy of a postcolonial art in solidarity with a leftist cause was abstract form, which was considered a European imposition and the epitome of individual expression. Such convictions prospered at a time when the Iraqi government also had strong economic and cultural ties with the Soviet Union, and student exchanges as well as traveling exhibitions between Iraq and Soviet states were common.

These realist currents are apparent in Siti's student work from this period. Siti's medium of printmaking was in itself an act of solidarity as it was considered a leftist practice promoted by socialist countries. His heavy black-and-white woodblock prints depict representational scenes of universal human suffering, such as prisoners, war and sickness. Besides a few portraits of his family, Siti rarely referenced specific markers of his geographic or social context. Not only did he want to relate his work to a global movement, but he and the other art students feared retribution from the government if any of their work was too specifically critical of the regime. In one of Siti's woodblock prints from his time at the Institute of Fine Arts in Baghdad, a distraught man crouches with his hands tied behind his back. The man's form is made from the negative white space of the print, which stands out starkly against the pitch-black ink of the background. His figure fills the composition, pressed against the foreground, so that the viewer cannot look away from his suffering. At the same time, Siti's staccato zigzagging lines across the contours of the man's body to denote shadow also dissolve the edges of the man's white form into the black background. As in his <u>Dialogue of Towers III</u> (2013), Siti's forms create a tension between overwhelming presence and disappearance.

One cannot help but correlate this universal representation of subjugation with the way in which Siti's hands were metaphorically tied by his social condition. While Siti and his fellow students tried to embed their work in a universal leftist art movement, they were often limited by government censorship, quickly-changing loyalties, and in Siti's case, mistreatment of Kurds. The Iraqi government's relationship to leftist causes fluctuated from promotion to persecution constantly throughout Siti's time in Baghdad.

Siti's hands were also tied by the feeling that his teachers were too conservative. Despite the correspondence between representational painting and leftist movements among young Iraqi art students of the 1970s, figural painting still had a strong link to the European academic painting tradition in the art schools of Baghdad. Siti's teachers had all trained at the big art academies in Europe, such as Paris, Rome and London, and many of them still believed that academic methods of painting, such as using scientific perspective to make representational landscapes or nudes, was the best form of art training.

Several decades before Siti and other young artists in the 1970s questioned their practice's belonging to global art movements, Iraqi artists in the immediate postcolonial period of the 1950s were grappling with their own sense of belonging to European culture and exile from their own through colonial legacies. Siti references T.S. Eliot's poem The Waste Land in his 2016 work A Wasteland and two sculptural works from 2017, Phantom Land and Floodland, in which monochrome lattices of raised geometric forms cover amorphous wooden hardboard cut-outs. In the 1950s, T.S. Eliot was central to Iraqi discussions on how to navigate the postcolonial dilemma of a national art production. The Iraqi poet Badr Shakir al-Sayyab (1926–1964) wrote in the early 1950s: 'Have you read what T.S. Eliot said of the individual talent and tradition and their relation to poetry? … Our poetry should not be a mimic of the West in Arab or semi-Arab attire. Let us make use of the best in our poetic tradition while making use of the achievements of Western writers.'[3] Throughout this 1950s discourse is a tone of hopefulness, a feeling that certain forms related to Iraqi or Arab tradition could lead to a unique local modern culture. But like Siti's towers, such binary thinking as 'Arab and Western tradition' excluded many other forms of thinking. Kurds and other ethnic minorities were often left behind in the pan-Arab movements prominent in Iraqi nationalism. The Malwiya minaret itself was associated in modern Iraq with the pinnacle of Arab culture in the early centuries of Islam, and the ladder was connected with a so-called traditional Iraqi stone and mudbrick home, where ladders were used for centuries to reach the roof where people would sleep to escape the heat.

Seen from this historical perspective, these symbols' appearance in Siti's later work are not just references to a lost geographic homeland but to the negotiations of belonging and nationhood prevalent within the artistic communities he inhabited in Baghdad in the 1970s. Throughout his practice since his exile to London, Siti inverts the hopefulness and inclusivity of these symbols. While all of Siti's central forms facilitate upward movement, his works repeatedly remind us that such a constant upward striving can be dangerous and egotistical, leading to violence, destruction and discrimination. Towers must necessarily taper to a point in order to stand, where fewer can climb, leaving many at the bottom. In Elusive Mountain (2018), Siti transforms the metaphorical dangers of climbing into physical pain by creating a mountain form from barbed wire against a limestone background. His installation at Al Riwaq Gallery in Bahrain Right to Climb (2017) embeds ladders at oblique and divergent angles from one another across a series of cubes, so that despite the ladders' formal promise of upward movement, Siti's composition precludes the viewer from climbing. Across his practice, these elements are also stripped of a social context that artists in 1970s Baghdad claimed to mirror through the ideology of realism. Instead, the forms of the symbols serve as building blocks for his own internal meditations on the social contexts surrounding these topographies in relation to Siti himself.

Artistic networks in Iraq overcame the exclusionary discourse – as Siti repeatedly reminds, there was a solidarity among them that bypassed nationalist or pan-Arab politics. However, as the Ba'th government's persecution of the Kurds and other minorities and insistence on party allegiance became increasingly strong in the 1970s, it became impossible to avoid national politics within the art schools of Baghdad. In order not to join the Ba'th party, a requirement for entering the next level of art school in Baghdad, Siti moved with a few friends to Yugoslavia, where the Iraqi government had strong ties. After a brief stay in Belgrade, Siti and his fellow artists had to leave again for Ljubljana, where they would not have to pay university fees.

There, Siti felt at once a creative liberation and a deep alienation. He and his fellow Iraqi students went there looking for a universal realism embedded in leftist ideology that would encompass all global art movements. Instead, Siti was surprised to find experimentation with different forms, and especially media, which he found intensely liberating for his artistic practice. He continued to work in printmaking but he experimented with colour, silkscreen and collage. In his silkscreen series Current (1980), he inlays newspaper and book clippings into an abstract grid of multi-coloured squares whose composition hints at dossiers of criminal investigations. A bar of music punctuates the centre of each print. While diverging from his previous practice in Baghdad, these prints followed Siti's Slovenian teachers' work closely. Despite being suddenly given the freedom to experiment, Siti felt a need as an outsider to belong and be accepted at the school in Ljubljana by keeping close to the work of others around him.

He also continued to strive for a belonging in another sense in his work from this period. In his Ljubljana silkscreens, Siti had the freedom, away from the Ba'th regime, to openly criticise the situation in Iraq through the inclusion of contemporary newspaper clippings. Yet, these forms were still based on the necessity of collectivity in art that did not allow for individual expression. Siti writes: 'At the same time I was still heavily influenced by Iraqi policy, I still felt like … a slave to a very rigid ideology in art, that held that art should be consistently in the service of society … that art holds a primarily utilitarian function.'

This collective critique of the Iraqi regime eventually had consequences outside of Siti's artistic practice. At the start of the Iran–Iraq War in September 1980, the close diplomatic ties between Yugoslavia and Iraq meant that the Iraqi regime began persecuting dissenters in Ljubljana. Siti was pursued by the Yugoslavian police – his work was removed from exhibitions, his home was ransacked and he was beaten. The violence he had run away from had pursued him and he was forced into exile again, this time to London after several other rejections for refugee status. He has remained in London ever since.

So we return, as the poet al-Bayati prophesied, to the wound, to London, and to the images of the Malwiya frenetically scribbled by Siti across the barren landscape of a telephone bill. It was Siti's geographic return, his eventual visit home to Duhok after the Gulf War in 1991, that transformed this frantic practice laden with trauma into a simplified abstraction around a small sample of images derived from the Iraqi landscape. It was the physical violence and destruction of the society and landscape and the distance from it imposed on him that urged him towards creative individualism. While his physical homecoming may have been the impetus, his formal shift was not an attempt at the resurrection of a lost place or time.

He had never climbed the Malwiya, nor had it featured in his artistic career up to that point. More importantly, recreation of geographic place would be dishonest, as Siti never had such a place to belong to, even as a child in Duhok, and to disappear into such an imagined homeland would not do justice to the pain inflicted on both himself and his society.

Instead, Siti's poetic monochrome abstractions, repeated variations on themes inspired from topographic markers in Iraq, are tools to reach the core of Siti's internal struggle. By tracing his own wounds, he links them to those of others – a constellation built on pain, but through its very form, its interconnectedness, implying hope.

In a corner of his studio, Walid Siti has dismembered a dead tree from his garden, built a lattice from its branches by bonding them together with twist ties used for groceries or gardening, and imposed this reticulation on the tree's upside-down root system. It is not so much the impossible verticality of an inverted tree that one notices but the crude joints, incidental angles, and the multifarious generations of negative space through the branches and their shadows. As the novelist Olga Tokarczuk wrote: 'constellation, not sequencing, carries truth.'[4]

1
Translated in: Muhsin Jassim al-Musawi, "Abd al-Wahhab al-Bayati's Poetics of Exile," in: Journal of Arabic Literature 32:2 (2001): 212–38, 215.

2
Dia al-Azzawi, et.al., "Towards a New Vision (Baghdad, 1969)." Translated in Anneka Lenssen, Sarah Rogers and Nada Shabout, eds., Modern Art in the Arab World: Primary Documents (New York: The Museum of Modern Art, 2018), 306–9.

3
Muhsin J. al-Musawi, Arabic Poetry: Trajectories of modernity and tradition (London: Routledge, 2006), 108.

4
Olga Tokarczuk, Flights, Jennifer Croft trans. (London: Fitzcarraldo Editions, 2018), 83.

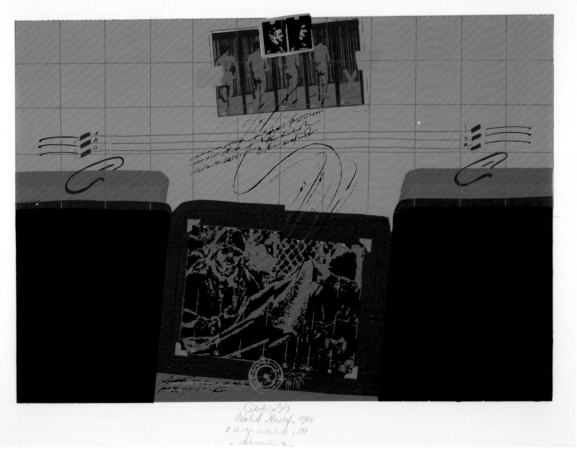

Current series, 1980. Silkscreen prints on paper. 50 × 70 cm.

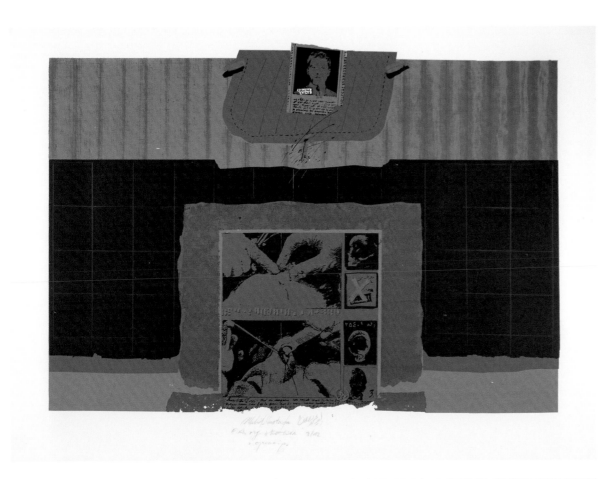

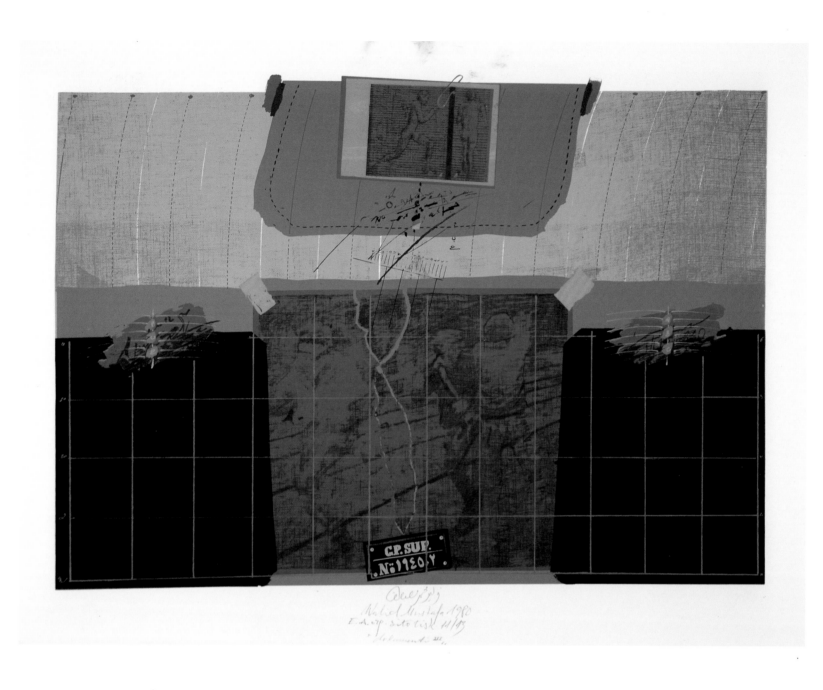

Current series, 1980. Silkscreen prints on paper. 50 × 70 cm.

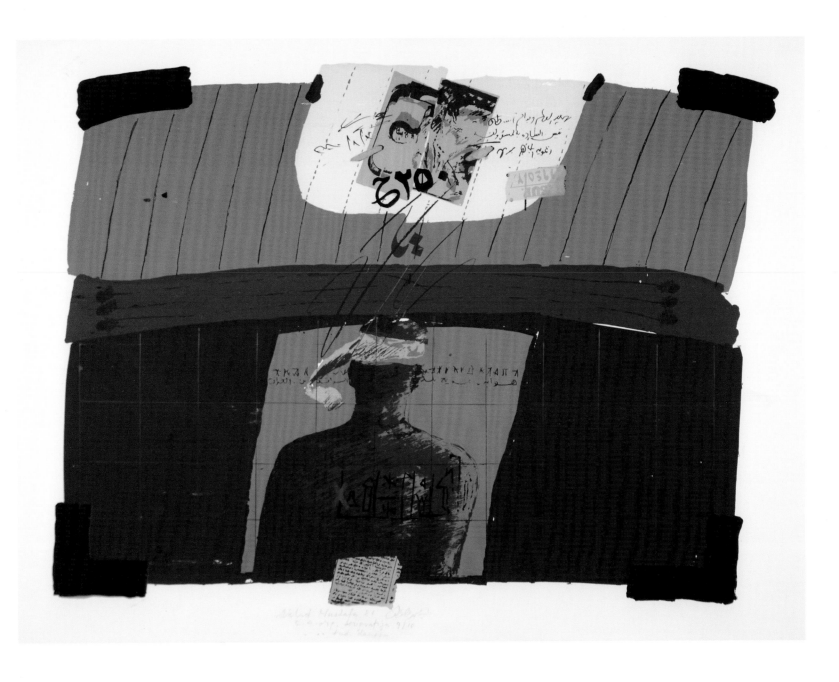

153

Right to Climb, 2017. Site-specific installation. Timber and paint. 800 × 120 × 120 cm.
Nest public art event, Al Riwaq Gallery, Bahrain, 2017. Photo credit: Sheenwar Siti.

Passage, 2016. C-print. 89 × 59 cm.

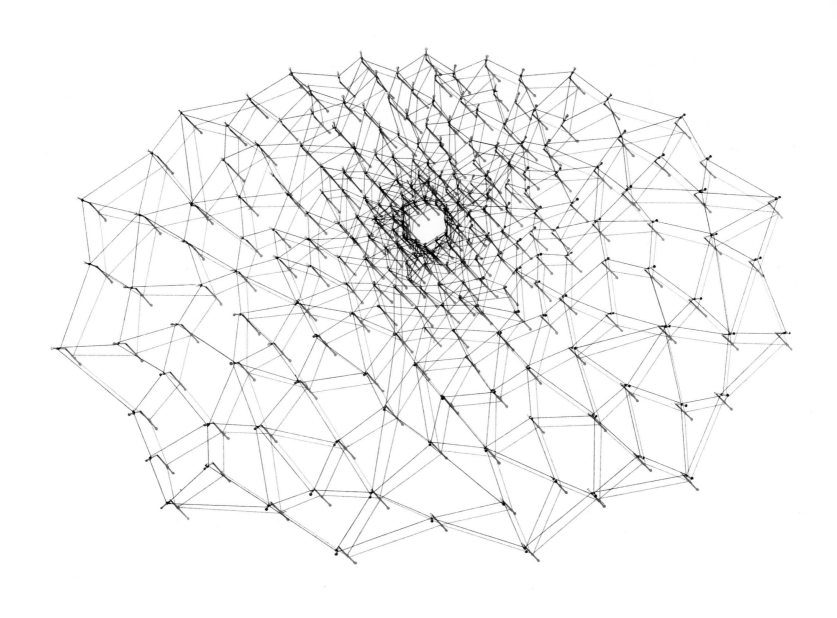

A Perfect Formation, 2012. Wall-based installation. Nails and thread on MDF. 24 × 320 × 8 cm.
Group exhibition *Systems and Patterns* at the International Centre for Graphic Arts, Ljubljana, 2012.

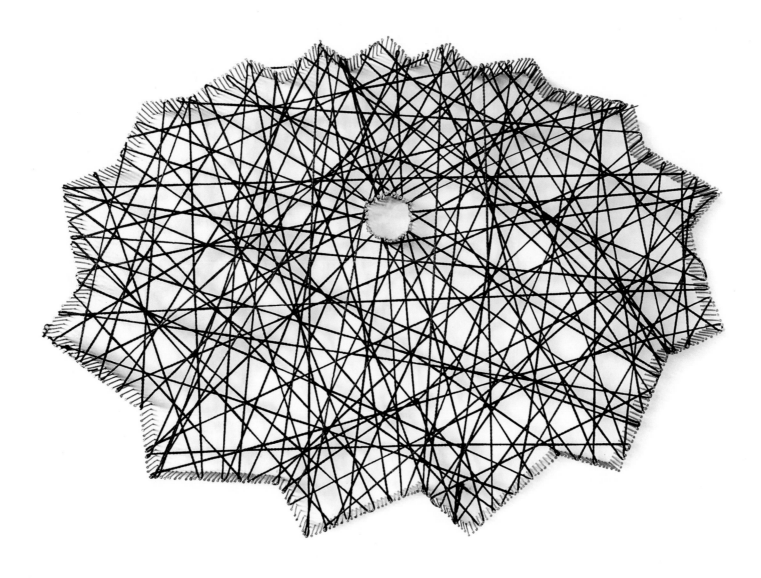

A Perfect Formation II, 2012. Thread and nails on MDF board. Size variable.

Constellation, 2009. Board, emulsion paint, plaster, thread and nails. 250 × 480 × 25 cm.
Group exhibition *Planet K* at 53rd International Venice Biennale, 2009.

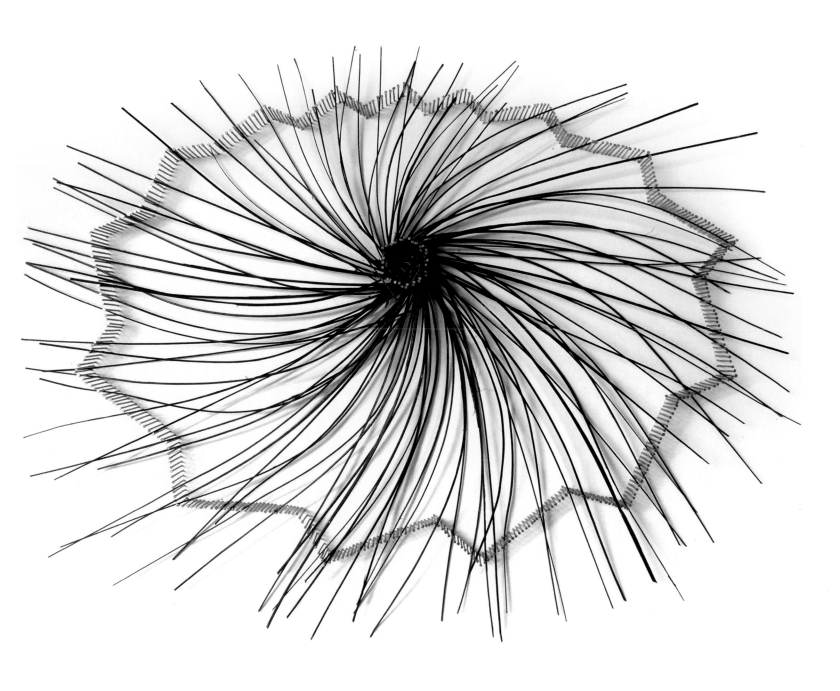

A Perfect Formation III, 2012. Thread and nails on MDF board. Size variable.

Sketch for *The White Cube* series, 2010. Graphite on paper. Both works 30 × 42 cm.

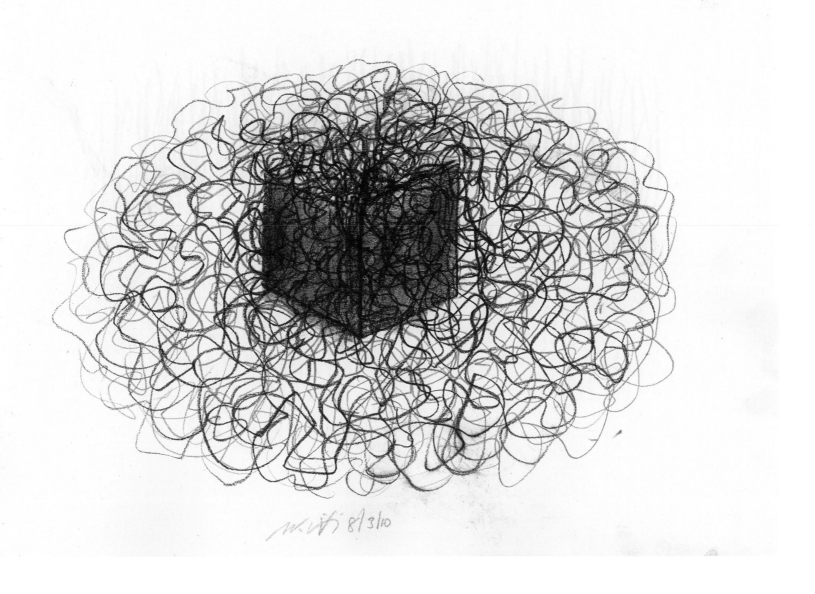

Sketch for *The White Cube* series, 2010. Charcoal and pencil on paper. 30 × 42 cm.
Sketch for *The White Cube* series, 2010. Graphite on paper. 30 × 42 cm.

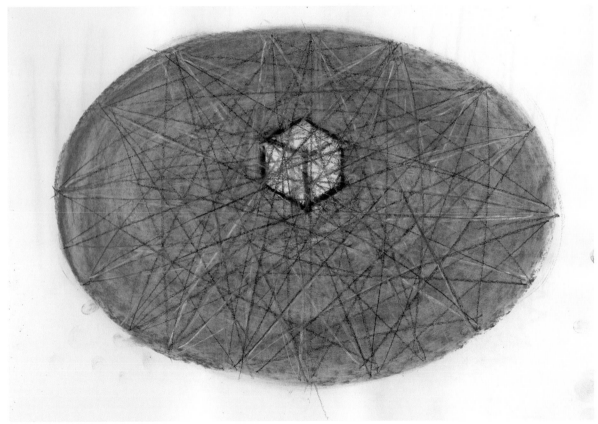

Sketch for *The White Cube* series, 2010. Crayon and charcoal on paper. 30 × 42 cm.
Sketch for *The White Cube* series, 2010. Charcoal and ink on paper. 30 × 42 cm.

Sketch for *The White Cube* series, 2010. Charcoal and pencil on paper. 30 × 42 cm.

The White Cube series, 2010. Pastel on paper. 68 × 110 cm.

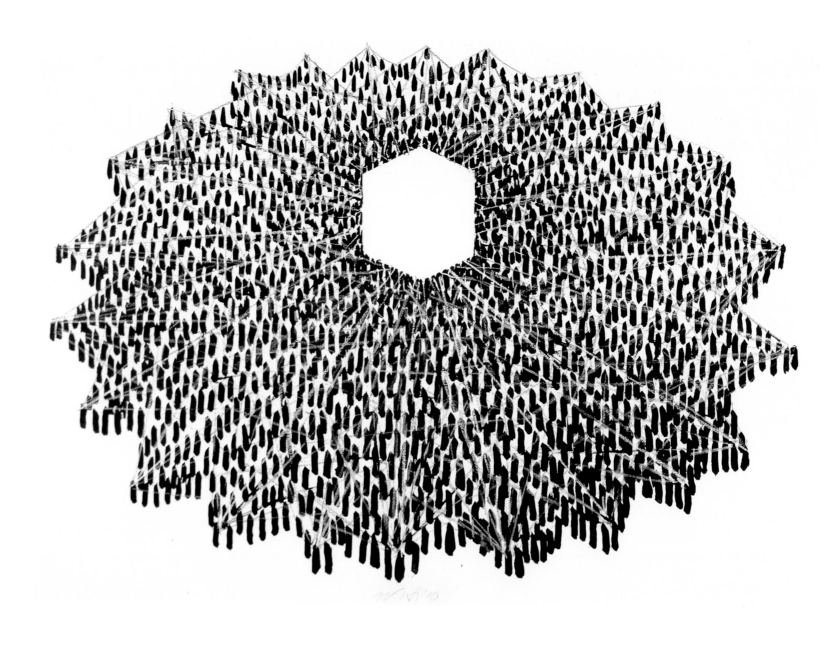

The White Cube series, 2010. Crayon and ink on paper. 68 × 110 cm.

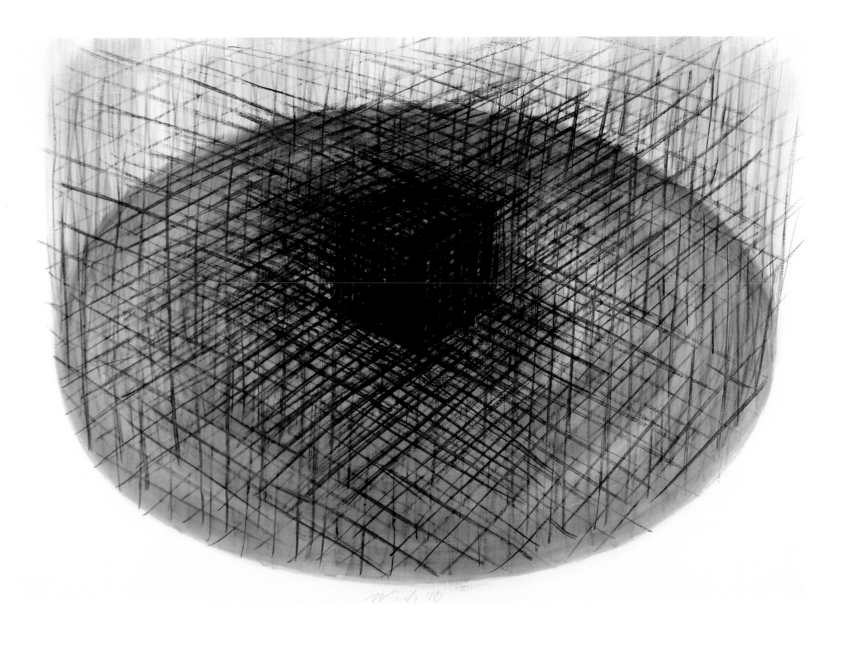

The White Cube series, 2010. Acrylic and charcoal on paper. 68 × 110 cm.

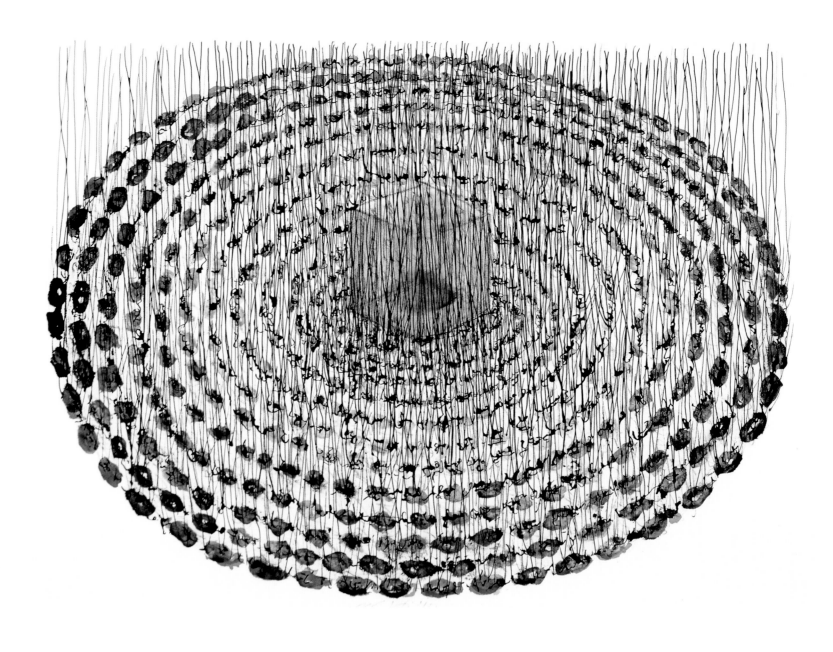

The White Cube series, 2010. Ink on paper. 68 × 110 cm.

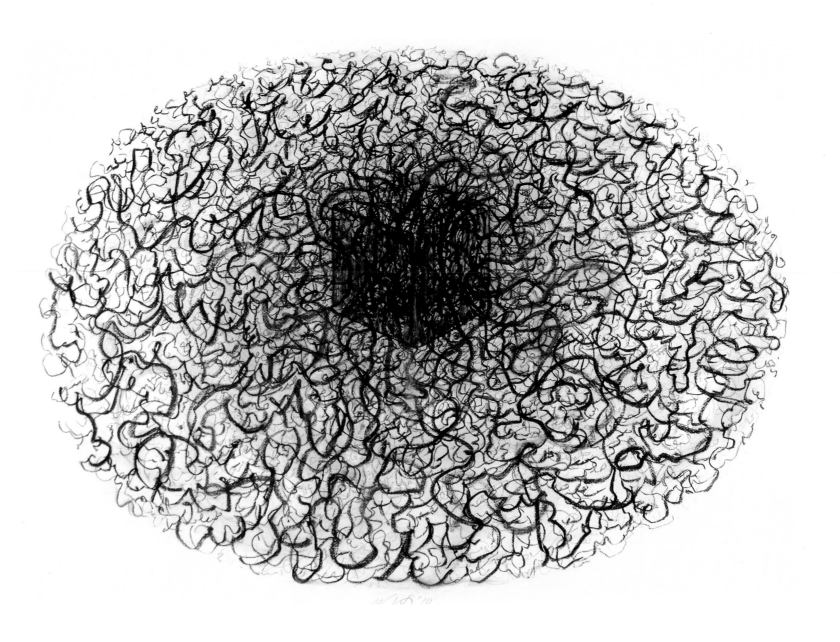

The White Cube series, 2010. Crayon on paper. 68 × 110 cm.

The White Cube series, 2010. Charcoal and crayon on paper. 68 × 110 cm.
Courtesy of the Trustees of the British Museum 2011, 6014.1. (Funded by CaMMEA acquisitions group).

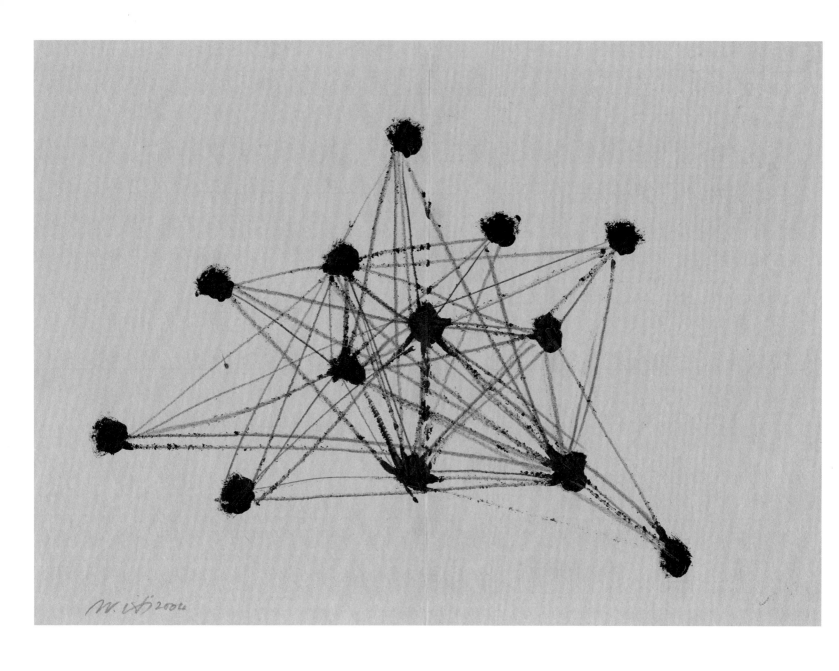

Family Ties series, 2004. Acrylic, crayon and graphite on paper. 32 × 42 cm.

Family Ties series, 2004. Acrylic and graphite on paper. 32 × 42 cm.

Family Ties series, 2004. Acrylic and graphite on paper. 32 × 42 cm.

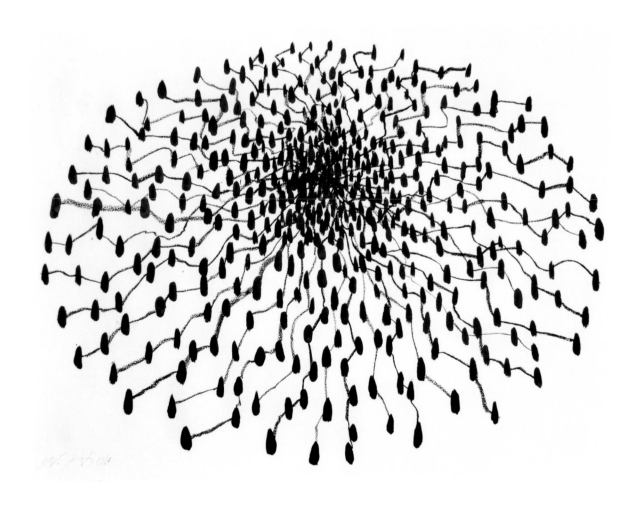

Family Ties series, 2004. Acrylic and pastel on paper. 56 × 76 cm.

Family Ties series, 2004. Acrylic and crayon on paper. 56 × 76 cm.

New Mountains, 2011. Acrylic on paper. 56 × 76 cm.

The Fall II, 2011. Acrylic on paper. 74 × 165 cm.

Shifting Domain, 2013. Acrylic and crayon on paper. 64 × 94 cm.

Dialogue of Towers I, 2013. Acrylic on canvas. 211 × 260 cm.

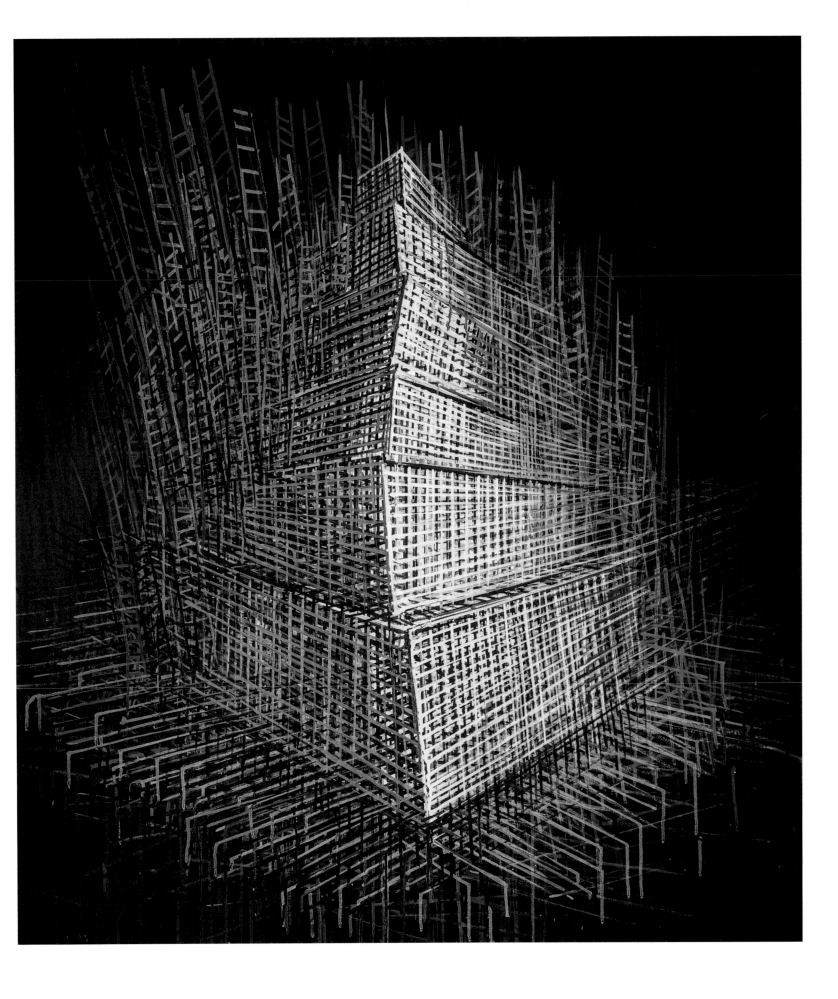

Dialogue of Towers III, 2013. Acrylic on canvas. 126 × 111 cm.
Photo credit: Heini Schneebli.

Walid Siti
b. 1954, Dohuk, Kurdistan-Iraq
Lives and works in London

Education

1982 MA and BA, Academy of Fine Arts,
Ljubljana, Slovenia
1976 Diploma in printmaking, Institute of Fine Arts,
Baghdad, Iraq

Selected Solo Exhibitions

2017 The Black Tower, Zilberman Gallery, Berlin
2015 New Babylon, Zilberman Gallery, Istanbul, Turkey
2014 Re-Construction, Edge of Arabia, London, UK
Parallel Realms, Taymour Grahne Gallery,
New York, USA
2013 Amed Art Gallery, Diyarbakır, Turkey
2011 Rose Issa Projects, London, UK
Erbil–Dubai: Chasing Utopia, XVA Gallery, Dubai, UAE
Merg Gallery, Erbil, Kurdistan-Iraq
2010 Sardem Gallery, Sulaymaniyah, Kurdistan-Iraq
Dohuk Gallery, Dohuk, Kurdistan-Iraq
2009 XVA Gallery, Dubai, UAE
2008 Leighton House Museum, London, UK
2004 Salman's Gallery, Dohuk, Kurdistan-Iraq
2002 Arcola Gallery, London, UK
2001 Oriel Canfas, Cardiff, UK
1998 Diorama Gallery, London, UK
1996 Leighton House Museum, London, UK
1992 Midland Arts Centre, Birmingham, UK

Selected Group Exhibitions

2020 Rencontres Internationales Paris / Berlin, France
and Germany
When Globe Means Home: This Is Our Story,
Gallerie delle Prigioni, Treviso, Italy
2019 Refuge and Renewal: Migration and British Art,
Royal West Academy Gallery, Bristol, UK
Speaking Across Mountains, Middle East Institute,
Washington D.C., USA
Impossible to Find, Latitude Gallery Art Space,
Yerevan, Armenia
History Is Not Here: Art and the Arab Imaginary,
Minnesota Museum of American Art, Saint Paul,
USA
1st Public Art Duhok 2019, Duhok, Kurdistan-Iraq
Hammams' Maqam, 3rd Kurdistan Sound Art
Exhibition, Duhok, Kurdistan-Iraq
2018 Pay Attention Please!, Public Art Amsterdam,
Amsterdam, Netherlands
The Arrangements of the Soul in the Universe,
Langen Foundation, Yogyakarta, Indonesia
Infinite Present: Revelations from Islamic Design in
Contemporary Art, Cambridge Arts, Cambridge, USA
International Contemporary Art Exhibition, Yerevan,
Armenia
Baghdad Mon Amour, Institute of Cultures of Islam
(ICI) Paris, France
2017 Age of Terror: Art since 9/11, The Imperial War
Museum, London, UK
Tamawuj, the 13th Sharjah Biennale, Sharjah, UAE
House of Wisdom, Framer Framed, Amsterdam,
Netherlands
2016 Visions of War Above and Below, The Imperial War
Museum, London, UK
Ultra Habitat, Zilberman Gallery, Berlin, Germany
Restrictions of the Earth, Karşı Sanat Çalışmaları,
Istanbul, Turkey
Restrictions of the Earth, Hinterland Gallery, Vienna,
Austria
2015 Arab Territories, Capital of Arab Culture 2015,
Constantine, Algeria
Between East and West, Yinchuan Museum of
Contemporary Art (MOCA), Yinchuan, China
The Air of Earth, ArtBat Festival, Almaty,
Kazakhstan
The Great Game, Pavilion of Iran, 56th Venice
Biennale, Venice, Italy
Bruges Triennial, Belgium
2014 The Seven Valleys, Rose Issa Projects, London, UK

2013 In Dialogue, The Waterline Gallery, Manama, Bahrain
Iran Modern, Asia Society, New York, USA
Hajj: Journey to Mecca, Museum of Islamic Art, Doha, Qatar

2012 Systems and Patterns, International Centre of Graphics, Ljubljana, Slovenia
Hajj: Journey to the Heart of Islam, British Museum, London, UK
Silent Revolution: Tallinn Drawing Triennial, Tallinn Art Hall, Tallinn, Estonia
Echoes from Periphery, Palazzo Granafei Nervegna, Brindisi, Italy

2011 Pavilion of Iraq, 54th Venice Biennale, Venice, Italy
Take Care of Yourself, Amed Art Gallery, Diyarbakır, Turkey

2009 Taswir: Pictorial Mappings of Modernity and Islam, Martin-Gropius-Bau, Berlin, Germany
Planet K, Kurdish Collateral Event, 53rd Venice Biennale, Venice, Italy
Iraq's Past Speaks to the Present, British Museum, London, UK
Modernism and Iraq, Miriam & Ira Wallach Art Gallery, Columbia University, New York, USA

2008 Permanent Collection, Imperial War Museum, London, UK
Occupied Space 08, Art for Palestine, Qattan Foundation, London, UK
18th Istanbul International Art Fair, Istanbul, Turkey
Space Now, The Triangle, London, UK

2006 Word into Art, The British Museum, London, UK

2004 Art Futures, Contemporary Arts Society, London, UK
Commemorating Serwat Anawr, The Museum Hall, Sulaymaniyah, Iraq

2003 Still Packing Suitcases, Limonaia di Villa Strozzi, Florence, Italy
Outlook, The National Museum in Krakow, Poland

2002 Kurdish Contemporary Art, The Historical Museum of The City of Vienna, Austria
10th Asian Art Biennale, Dhaka, Bangladesh

2001 5th Sharjah Biennale, Sharjah, UAE
International Art Biennale Dialogue, St. Petersburg, Russia

2000 Thing, The Garret Centre, London, UK

1999 The 9th International Biennale of Prints and Drawings, Taiwan, China
XIV Premio Internazional Biella per l'incisione, Biella, Italy

Towards the Millennium, Artsway, Hampshire, UK
Pilonava Galeria, Ajdovščina, Slovenia

1998 Cheltenham Open Drawing '98 touring to Hall and Berlin, Germany

1997 The 8th International Biennale of Prints and Drawings, Taiwan, China

1996 10th International Exhibition of Graphic Art, Frechen, Germany
Contemporary Art Collection, Imperial War Museum, London, UK
Under Different Skies, Oksenhallen, Copenhagen, Denmark

1995 Graphic Constellation '95, Graz, Austria

1994 Print Triennale '94, Consumenta 95, Nuremberg, Germany
International Print Triennale, Kraków, Poland
Scarborough Art Gallery, Scarborough, UK

1993 The First International Print Biennale, Maastricht, Netherlands
Greenwich Citizen Gallery, London, UK

1992 Kelvingrove Art Gallery and Museum, Glasgow, UK

1991 Castle Museum, Nottingham, UK
South Bank Centre, London, UK
The Bluecoat, Liverpool, UK
Aberystwyth Arts Centre, Aberystwyth, UK

1987 Print with a Point, Hard Time Gallery, Bristol, UK

1986 Three Iraqi Artists, Kufa Gallery, London, UK

1983 15th International Graphics Biennale, Ljubljana, Slovenia

Public Collections

The Metropolitan Museum of Art, New York, USA
Museum of Contemporary Art, Kraków, Poland
Sharjah Art Foundation, Sharjah, UAE
The British Museum, London, UK
Victoria and Albert Museum, London, UK
The Imperial War Museum, London, UK
Art in Embassies Program, USA
The World Bank, Washington D.C., USA
The Iraq Memory Foundation, Baghdad, Iraq and Washington D.C., USA
Barjeel Art Foundation, Sharjah, UAE
The National Gallery of Amman, Jordan

The artist expresses his sincere appreciation to his beloved wife and two sons for their ongoing support and assistance. He also wishes to thank Rose Issa for her generous support throughout his career and for this project in particular, and Iraqi artists Dia al-Azzawi and the late Mahmoud Sabri for their kind continuing support throughout the years.

This publication has been made possible with the generous support of the Makiya-Kufa Gallery Trust and the Arab Fund for Arts and Culture.

AFAC ARAB FUND FOR
ARTS AND CULTURE
الصـــندوق العــربي
للثقـــافة والفنـــون

© 2020 Kehrer Verlag Heidelberg Berlin, Walid Siti and authors

Editor: Nat Muller
Texts: Zainab Bahrani, Sarah Johnson, Nat Muller, Venetia Porter
Project Management: Kehrer Verlag (Sylvia Ballhause)
Copyediting: Nat Muller
Proofreading: Petra Joswig
Design: Studio Victor Balko
Image Processing: Kehrer Design (Erik Clewe)
Production Management: Kehrer Design (Tom Streicher)

Cover Illustration: *Ceremonies*, 2016. Plastic figurines and straw. 40 × 40 × 40 cm.

Chapter Illustrations:
War + Conflict (pp. 18/19): *The Great Game*. Installation detail. The Iranian Pavilion at the 56th Venice Biennale, 2015.
Landscape + Architecture (pp. 72/73): Installation view *Phantom Land*, 2017. Hard board, foam board, plaster of Paris, grout and acrylic paint. 5 × 700 × 900 cm. 13th Sharjah Biennale *Tamawuj*, Sharjah, 2017. Courtesy of the Sharjah Art Foundation.
Belonging + Exile (pp. 142/143): *War* series, 1986. Ink on paper. 24 × 29 cm.

Bibliographic information published by the Deutsche Nationalbibliothek: The Deutsche Nationalbibliothek lists this publication in the Deutsche Nationalbibliografie; detailed bibliographic data is available on the Internet at dnb.dnb.de.

Printed and bound in Germany
ISBN 978-3-86828-927-5

 Kehrer Heidelberg Berlin
www.kehrerverlag.com